MORE THAN MUSIC

STEPHEN PHIFER

Becoming a Highly Effective Worship Team

Hayley, You are such a blessing to
Petra, and to the Worship Ministry!
Thank You for allowing the Holy
Spirit to flow through You!
God Bless, Calvt Godyear
John 4:23

MORE THAN MUSIC

STEPHEN PHIFER

Becoming a Highly Effective Worship Team

Empowered Publications, Inc
Millry, Alabama

Published by:
Filled Books
An Imprint of Empowered Publications Inc.
529 County Road 31
Millry, Alabama 36558

Library of Congress Control Number: 2018946288

ISBN: 978-1-943033-70-6 (paperback)
ISBN: 978-1-943033-71-3 (eBook)
ISBN: 978-1-943033-72-0 (cloth hardcover)

Dedication

For all the singers, instrumentalists, technicians, and their leaders who do the work of worship in their own hearts and in their churches. May Psalm 50:2 be your experience, "Out of Zion, the perfection of beauty, God will shine forth."

Acknowledgments

So many people have helped make this book a reality. First, my wife, Freeda, whose belief in me never wavers. She has been a constant encouragement. My daughters and their husbands, Rev. Matt and Nicole Huett, and Manny and Jennifer Foret are always a blessing. Like a sister to me, my cousin, Nancy Hopkins Howie, is my go-to-reader who never refuses to let me read something to her over the phone. The idea for the book came from a student of mine, Rev. Caleb Gudgeon. These minister friends helped me greatly along the way: John Gifford, Bob Brock, Randy Brock, Danny Austin, and Charlie Perkins. My proofreader, Becky Burton was a tremendous help as were a host of young worship leaders on the Assemblies of God Music Minister Facebook page. I think we made a "highly effective team!" Thanks!

Endorsements

Worship is famously described as the source and summit of the entire Christian life. Everything flows from worship and conduces to it. *More than Music: Becoming a Highly Effective Worship Team* provides a good starting point for the critical task of studying worship from a biblical and Christ-centered perspective, gaining knowledge and wisdom regarding the work that followers of Jesus will be doing for eternity. It is difficult not to see the God-loving heart of Dr. Steve Phifer in this book. His deepest desire is for his heart (and the reader's heart) to resonate with the heart of God and his love for all of creation. ~ **Dr. James R. Hart, President, The Robert E. Webber Institute for Worship Studies.**

Dr. Phifer has written a book that will benefit anyone involved in any way in worship leading. He does not get bogged down in the "worship wars" that plague many congregations. Rather he develops theology that should inform everyone's approach to how we will lead congregations before God. ~ **Dr. Bob Caldwell. Theologian-in-Residence, Network 21, Professor of Theology, Global University.**

Having already read Dr. Phifer's book, *Worship that Pleases God*, I was itching to find out what he had installed for *More than Music*. Needless to say, I was not disappointed. Steve has a strong passion for worship, music, and scripture that he has been able to articulate well as written teachings for worship leaders, musicians, singers, and worshipers of any background. If you are looking for a resource that helps explain what praise and worship is and what it can look like as a leader and team member, in layman's terminology, including lots of scriptural references, look no further. ~ **Luke Gambill. Assistant Professor of Music/ Coordinator of Contemporary Worship, William Carey University.**

Stephen Phifer has written a concise, deeply spiritual and practical book on biblical foundations and practical applications of worship that every pastor, staff member, worship team leader and member should read, study and apply. His work skillfully shows us how to experience "worship in spirit and truth" (John 4:24) both privately and in public worship as prescribed by Jesus.

Like Dr. Phifer, my doctorate is also in the field of worship studies. His book, however, has revealed principles and practices that will be transformational for me personally and for my church, as he has called us back to our first love and first calling to love the Lord our God with all our heart, soul, and mind (Matt. 22:37). His work has challenged and encouraged me to put as a priority (personally and corporately) the entering in to God's presence in the holy place where "with unveiled face, beholding as in a mirror the glory of the Lord, (we) are being transformed into the same image from glory to glory, just as by the Spirit of the Lord" (2 Cor. 3:18). ~ **The Reverend Dr. Danny Austin, Pastor, The Oaks Church, Gainesville, Florida.**

Steve, just finished your new book. It is absolutely excellent. The way you approach the generational dynamics utilizing "Polarizing terms" is genius and how you connect that with the fabric of God's created universe is eye opening. The mark of a good book in my mind is that it makes me think rather than tell me what to think. You have hit the nail on the head with this. ~ **Pastor Randy Brock, Lead Care Pastor, Victory Church, Lakeland, FL.**

More Than Music is a finely articulated resource that explains Biblical principles and explores the various polarities of worship. It is perfect for teaching and studying God's Word to obtain a biblical understanding of worship. Whether you are a worship leader, worship team member, or a fellow worship participator, you will walk away with a greater understanding of personal and public worship. Practical takeaways make this a wonderful book to read with your worship team! ~ **Caleb Gudgeon Worship Director Trinity Assembly of God West Chester, Pennsylvania.**

I have had the privilege of reading this book, manual, and guideline that should be required reading for all worships leaders as well as all members of worship teams. What we do in a service on Sunday is useless unless it has been preceded by 6 days of worship. This work will help you guide yourself and your team, in a Godly biblical study of worship. I am also blessed to call Steve Phifer my first music pastor who taught me band, orchestra, directing, choir and worship leading; he helped shaped me my life for ministry. What is such a blessing, is that he has lived this all his life. This book is a culmination of worship, study, and application. My prayer is that the Body of Christ will get ahold of it and let the biblical teachings shape and change how worship is done. He states in his Book, "Because when we worship God here on earth, we are actually joining the constant worship of heaven. What a privilege!" ~ **Pastor Robb Stancer Creative Arts Pastor Brightmoor Christian Church, Detroit Michigan.**

With this book, Steve Phifer's practical wisdom and experience have moved from the keyboard of the piano to the keyboard of the computer. As countless churches have been blessed by his musical gifts as many will be instructed by his teaching in *More than Music.* ~ **Dr. Lester Ruth, Research Professor of Christian Worship, Duke Divinity School, Durham, North Carolina.**

Dr. Phifer shares from a lifetime of leading congregations in worship and teaching others on the theology of worship. This book is both a theological study of worship and a practical exploration of leading worship in today's churches. This would be a great resource to go through as a team, and he has added questions at the end of each chapter for further discussion. There are many contradictory views of what worship "should be" in today's churches. Steve lays out these views as natural dualities and calls us to minister to every believer. ~ **Rev. Andrew Soerens, Worship Pastor Bethel Church, Temple, TX.**

Dr. Phifer sees worship on every page of scripture. And he skillfully helps us connect the dots between First and New Covenants as well as leads into imagining that connection in our contemporary worship life. Not just the dominant "How to" rubrics in such vogue these days, but the What? and the Why? and What for? essentials so needed if one is to be a biblical, complete, optimally effective and "wide awake" worshiper or worship leader. ~ **Dr. Darrell A. Harris, Vice-President of Spiritual Life and Dean of the Chapel, The Robert E. Webber Institute for Worship Studies.**

Contents

Preface

In *More than Music: Becoming a Highly Effective Worship Team*, I attempt to bring my life's work as a writer, biblical student, and experienced worship pastor to bear on the fundamental and perennial challenges of worship team ministry. Because worship is expressed by culture, these two things become almost inseparable in our thinking, but separate them we must. Culture is temporary, and worship is eternal; it is essential for an effective worship team to constantly monitor these differences. Toward this goal, I have written the book in two sections:

1. The Biblical Study of Worship, and

2. The Biblical Study of Worship Leading.

The biblical instructions and principles of worship are eternal and absolute, applicable to all cultures. The local praxis of worship leading is temporary and relative, applicable in one place at one time. I want to clearly set forth the differences between the two.

The Biblical Study of Worship

In the first half of the book, we explore biblical terminology and models of worship. The reader is introduced to the original biblical meanings of important worship terms:

• Worship in Spirit and Truth,

• Psalms, hymns, and spiritual songs, and

• Praise and worship.

Seven biblical models of worship are presented which illustrate vital and universal aspects of worship.

• The structure of worship,

- The identity of worshipers,
- The function of worshipers,
- The Throne of God in worship,
- The Office-place of God in worship, and
- The flow of the River of Life through worship.

The Biblical Study of Worship Leading

The second half of the book applies these truths to the ministry of the worship team. I do not speak to controversial issues in public worship. My goal is to make application of the biblical truths that have the power to solve these conflicts. This book is not about the style of music or of technical presentations. I want to point out the eternal things so that the temporary things can be clearly seen. This is my attempt to "prove all things and hold fast to the good." In this way, these biblical principles and instructions can be useful across cultural divides.

Topics explored in the second half of the book are:

- The Leadership of the Holy Spirit,
- The Heart of the True Worshiper,
- The Call of God to lead worship,
- Finding the Dynamic Center between competing demands,
- An Effective Prayer Life, and,
- Continuing the work of Worship Renewal into the next generation.

Becoming a Highly Effective Worship Team

This is more than a subtitle; it expresses my intention to produce a useful study to help worship leaders and worship team members do this ministry well. Being on the team should be a delight and not a burden. Problems plaguing worship teams can be solved as the Holy Spirit does His work through the application of the Word in our hearts.

Suggestions for Use

More than Music is designed as a 12-week study course. I have tried to write each chapter to be read by team members before the class session and then taught by the worship leader. At the close of each chapter, there are seven discussion statements/ questions to help the team process the truths presented.

Plans for Use:

- A 12 week Sunday School-type of class,

- A year-long monthly teaching fellowship,

- A personal study by each team member,

- Weekly chapter readings with rehearsal devotions discussing the end of the chapter study questions, and

- A supplemental text in college and seminar classrooms studying the ministry of the worship team and worship leader.

Prelude
Call to Worship

Psalm 29:1-2
Give unto the Lord, O ye mighty, give unto the Lord glory
and strength. Give unto the Lord the glory due unto his
name; worship the Lord in the beauty of holiness.

The call to worship has gone out to all of creation. From the birds of the air, to the beasts of the field, to men and women of high and low estate, to children with their profound innocence, to even the heavenly angels around the Throne of God and of the Lamb, all are called to blend their voices in an offering of worship to God. What is the measure of this offering? Not the standards of earth, not the dimensions of time or space, not even the silent meditations of the heart—none of these things goes deep enough or high enough or wide enough to enclose the glory of the Lord for they are all His handiwork. Each of these measures tells part but not all of the story, the story of the Glory. This Glory is the only legitimate measure of our worship. We are called to gauge our praise and worship by this standard, "The Glory due His name."

We do not judge our success or failure by the response of the people we lead in worship. To do so is to lower the standard of our efforts to those of what is popular or revered, new or old, innovative or traditional. These are temporary standards and are totally insufficient as measures of worship. A highly effective worship team is one through whom God's Spirit flows.

"The Glory Due His Name"—a Standard for a Lifetime

As worship leaders and worship team members, we need the highest standard. It will be an anchor for us when the winds of culture rise and change threatens our moorings. It will be

20

a comfort to us when our best efforts seem to fall to the floor without touching anyone. In times of "success" when those we lead in worship join with us in passion, this standard will be our encouragement. In times of "failure" when critics arise and question our heart and intentions, if this has been our standard, we can know that God knows our heart.

This little book is all about "the Glory due His name." We will explore the ministry of the worship team from two complimentary vantage points:

- The biblical study of worship, and
- The practical study of worship leading.

These two things are not the same. One is eternal and the other is a temporal use of the eternal. One is a fountain ever flowing with truth. The other is a river where the truth flows through our lives and the lives of those we lead. The highly effective team studies both of these topics.

The Only Hope

How important is worship team ministry? The only hope of the world is Jesus. He is the only hope for us, our families and friends, and for our family of faith. When we worship, Jesus walks among us.

PART ONE
WORSHIP

Psalm 95:6-7

*O come, let us worship and bow down:
let us kneel before the LORD our maker.
For he is our God;
and we are the people of his pasture,
and the sheep of his hand.*

Chapter One

WORSHIP and WORSHIP LEADING

> **Revelation 19:1**
> And after these things I heard a great voice of much people in heaven, saying, Alleluia; Salvation, and glory, and honour, and power, unto the Lord our God:
> **2 Chronicles 5:11-14**
> And it came to pass, when the priests were come out of the holy place: (for all the priests that were present were sanctified, and did not then wait by course: Also the Levites which were the singers, all of them of Asaph, of Heman, of Jeduthun, with their sons and their brethren, being arrayed in white linen, having cymbals and psalteries and harps, stood at the east end of the altar and with them an hundred and twenty priests sounding with trumpets.) It came even to pass, as the trumpeters and singers were as one, to make one sound to be heard in praising and thanking the Lord; and when they lifted up their voice with the trumpets and cymbals and instruments of musick, and praised the Lord, saying, For he is good; for his mercy endureth for ever: that then the house was filled with a cloud, even the house of the Lord; So that the priests could not stand to minister by reason of the cloud: for the glory of the Lord had filled the house of God.

INTRODUCTION

Eternity and Time

The two passages of scripture above describe the dual nature of worship and worship leading.

- The Revelation passage describes the eternal Throne of God and of the Lamb in heaven. The Glory of the Lord is a permanent feature, never fading, never increasing for it cannot, and never surpassed by any other glory. This eternal glory excites the worship of heavenly hosts.

- The passage from 2 Chronicles describes an event, a glorious moment when, in response to the preparation of worship leaders, the Glory of the Lord filled the newly completed House of God. This moment, as glorious as it was, soon passed. It stands now as a monument to the history of worship, as a lesson from which worship leaders can learn, and as a goal for worship leaders to pursue.

As we will explore in Chapter Two, worship happens at the intersection of time and eternity. Often when a person sets out to study worship, he or she actually ends up studying worship leading: songs, styles, technologies, service orders, and leadership techniques. We will seek to avoid that error for the first half of this book. The subject will be worship, not worship leading.

What will we study? The eternal things: Who God is; who people are; what God wants; what people need; how God wants to be approached; how people need to come before the Lord; the arts of worship; the heart of worship; the purpose of worship; and the power of worship. These things are changeless from age to age and from culture to culture. The better we know these things the more effective we will be as worship team members.

The Subject of Worship

For information about worship leading, one can go to contemporary sources: testimonies, videos, recordings, and the fellowship of other worship leaders. This is, of course, a healthy and productive thing to do. However, if we want to study worship itself, the primary source is the Bible. Fortunately, the Bible is all about worship!

- The first family feud was about worship and it ended in murder.

- At each critical moment in the earliest history of God and man, the Patriarchs built altars of worship.

- Moses demanded the freedom of the Israelites so they could go worship.

- The first four of the Ten Commandments are concerned with worship.

- In the times of the judges, God's blessings rained down on the people when their worship was right and their enemies conquered them when idols took the place of Jehovah.

- King Saul corrupted worship and it cost him his crown.

- King David restored the Ark to the center of the Nation, established corporate worship, and initiated the tradition of the Psalms.

- King Solomon built the Temple where the Glory of the Lord stopped the service.

- When the worship of Israel drifted into idolatry, God allowed pagans to conquer them.

- Reformers: prophets, priests, and kings rebuilt the Temple and re-established Old Covenant worship.

- Jesus brought a New Covenant of worship in spirit and truth, sealing it with His blood and resurrection.

- The Holy Spirit came into the church to lead worship in spirit and truth.

- The early church spread the gospel around their world by establishing places of worship in every land.

- In Revelation we see why worship is the theme of history—it is the permanent state and activity of heaven.

So in this study, the Bible will be our primary source of information. We will seek out eternal things. In the second half, we will continue to explore the wisdom of scripture on how we should prepare for those amazing moments when "the glory of the Lord fills the house of the Lord."

Understanding the Bible

We need to know how to process the truth found in scripture. How does the Bible teach us truths that are applicable to life today?

- The first method is by direct command. The Bible instructs us to do or not do things.

- Next, the Bible teaches truths by telling stories, both histories and the parables of Jesus.

- The Bible also teaches us by principles drawn from commands and narratives.

A passage of scripture can have a direct impact on the reader as an application which may or may not apply to others. Doctrines are broad streams of truth found in both the Old and New Testaments, in histories, in prophecies, and in psalms. We can apply a single verse to our lives but we cannot make a doctrine from it.

The Subject of Worship Leading

Each worship service happens in a specific time and place. That time and place exists within a particular cultural context. Just as the Tabernacle in the Wilderness was a movable place of worship, New Covenant worship—worship in spirit and truth— is portable worship. It has traveled to every corner of the world.

For twenty centuries believers have sought to worship God in spirit and truth. Based on this unity of purpose, an astounding variety of worship styles and services has come into being. This is the divine plan of God, a necessary plan if the church is to reach the whole world with the Gospel. For this reason, this book will not explore the cultural aspects of worship leading in any great detail. We will instead explore what the Bible has to say about managing our culture and subordinating it to the plan and purposes of God.

The church is commanded to come out of the world, to be in it but not of it. That means, that while we operate in a particular set of cultural languages (Music is a cultural language!) the church actually exists in opposition to the culture. We do not share the fallen values of this world. We are called to be a holy counterculture speaking the truth of God into the surrounding culture. This must be done with the force of two great powers:

1. The power of the Holy Spirit, and

2. The power of genuine love.

In the name of Jesus, we will affirm the truth where we find it spoken by the culture. When we encounter the lies of the enemy, we will lovingly present the truth of God.

The Jesus Story

Above all other considerations, to be highly effective, we must tell the Jesus story. As Paul said, we must never be ashamed of the Gospel of Christ—the Jesus Story! It is the power of God for salvation to all who believe. It must not be lost in our presentations, personalities, or plans. Great private worship exists inside the Jesus Story. Great public worship tells the Jesus Story every week. When this is our message, we have a positive impact on this hurting world. The culture around us does not need our music, our oratory, or our personalities—people need Jesus. The ministry of the Holy Spirit is to make Jesus real to people. To the believer, this is an encounter with the One who loves us most. To the unbeliever, it is a powerful witness to his/ her need for a Savior. When we truly worship in spirit and truth, Jesus, Himself, walks among us.

DISCUSSION QUESTIONS

1. How would you describe the differences between the study of worship and the study of worship leading?

2. Can you list more "eternal" things about God? More "temporary" things about worship?

3. What biblical studies of worship have you done?

4. How do you see the relationship between worship and culture?

5. How do you respond to the idea of the church being a holy counterculture?

6. Do you see The Jesus Story as the centerpiece of our worship?

True Worship is More than Music!

Chapter Two

THE FUNDAMENTAL
POLARITY

Psalm 100

Make a joyful shout to the Lord, all you lands! Serve the Lord
with gladness; Come before His presence with singing. Know
that the Lord, He is God; it is He who has made us, and not
we ourselves; we are His people and the sheep of His pasture.
Enter into His gates with thanksgiving, and into His courts
with praise. Be thankful to Him, and bless His name. For the
Lord is good; His mercy is everlasting, and His truth endures
to all generations.

INTRODUCTION

Human beings are creatures bound in time. Everything
about us is affected by the passing of time. All events unfold
in time; they have a beginning, a middle, and an end. This is
true of songs, worship services, ministry careers, and even our
very lives. God is the Creator. He exists outside of time for it is

His invention. He has neither a beginning, nor a middle, nor an ending. Minutes, hours, days, weeks, years, decades, centuries pass on earth but in heaven, there are no clocks or calendars. We cannot imagine what that kind of life is like. It is the fundamental mystery of the Incarnation of Christ that He laid aside eternal existence and entered into time. When, through the power of His Blood, we worship Him in Spirit and in Truth, we somehow taste of eternity, even in our time-bound state. These biblical concepts lead us to this remarkable statement.

Worship happens at the intersection of Time and Eternity.

The author of this statement is unknown but its truth is one upon which we can all agree. When we deal with worship we are dealing with time in the light of eternity. We express eternal truths with songs and half of every song is time.

Polarities

Just as the earth has a north pole and south pole, many aspects of life come to us as polarities—opposite truths that do not cancel each other out but both remain in force. Modern thinking rejects the concept of polarities—two opposites being true at the same time. Our instinct is to choose one or the other. The Bible is not a modern book. The ancient world into which the Bible was spoken welcomed polarities. Jesus' teaching is full of paradoxes:

- To find your life, lose it.
- To lead, you must be the servant.
- To be first, volunteer to be last.

Worship Polarities

The subjects of worship and worship leading are filled with polarities: Understanding the polarities of worship is fundamental to a functional life in worship and worship leading. The Fundamental Polarity of New Covenant worship is Spirit and Truth:

We must not choose to worship in one of these dimensions but in both of them. Here are some examples of worship polarities:

- Preparation and Performance
- Planning and Improvising
- Majesty and Intimacy
- Celebration and Solemnity
- Tradition and Innovation
- Scripture and Culture
- Skill and Anointing
- Eternal truth and Time-bound experiences

The Dynamic Center

It is folly to think that we must choose between these things as we lead worship. The truth is we must find a dynamic center between these opposite truths.

- We must engage our spirit according to the truth of God.
- We must prepare to lead worship and then perform our ministry when the time comes.
- We must carefully plan ahead of time and then be flexible in the service itself.
- We must stand in awe of the "otherness" of God and also enter into the "closeness" of Him.

- We must celebrate the Lord with great joy and at other times tremble before Him in silence.

- We must continue the holy traditions of worship from generation to generation and also sing a new song to the Lord.

- We must operate on a scriptural basis while speaking the languages of the culture in which we serve.

- God gives us talent which we develop into skill which can then be anointed by the Spirit.

- We must recognize the eternal character of God while we experience holy times of His visitation.

WORSHIP IS EXPERIENCED IN TIME

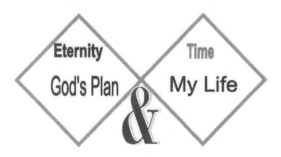

Worship and Culture

At the intersection of time and eternity, the interplay of worship and culture must be understood. Although rooted in eternal things, when worship is expressed, it is done so with temporal things. New Covenant worship is worship in spirit and truth, a highly adaptable force in the world. The eternal truths revealed in the Bible capture the hearts of worshipers in every land where the Gospel has gone. In those places, the worship services are shaped by the individual cultures. Eternal things shared by all believers take on different sounds and looks, tempos and emotions.

Unity with Diversity

With scripture as the unifying factor, the diversity of culture reminds one of the works of God in creation.

- The unity of design in all birds creates the astounding varieties of birdlife.
- The common environment of water supports the amazing underwater zoo of aquatic life.
- Vertebrate mammals share this common backbone but walk the earth in a myriad of species.

In the same way, a common theology underlies the diverse sounds and appearances of worship in the various cultures of the world.

Generational Cultures

Within these cultures, generational differences exert tremendous influence on how worship is expressed. Each culture of the world is made up of subcultures emerging from generation to generation. The survival of a culture in history is dependent upon the transfer of values from generation to generation. There is a verb used by worship scholars for this, "traditioning." It is defined as the process of passing values and beliefs on to the next generation. This process is essential to the health and survival of a civilization.

- Despite centuries of persecution and systematic violence, the Jewish people exist today because they have succeeded at traditioning.
- This is a primary concern of scripture and a primary function of worship.

Awareness of these truths stretches our understanding far beyond our own preferences. While it is natural for worshipers to judge all worship by their own experience, worship team members must serve others not just their own tastes. This must be done sincerely and not in a condescending way.

Generational Heart-Songs

Because of shared experience, generations within a culture develop their own tastes and preferences in music. This is evidenced by the variety of popular music tailored to various generations. People bring these preferences with them to God's house. Worship teams need to know the heart-songs of the people they intend to lead in worship.

- What is a heart-song? A heart-song is a particular set of styles of music which opens the heart of an individual. The heart-song is also distinguished by the content of the music. Certain textual themes and styles of language move certain generations.

- How can we determine a generation's heart-songs? Listen to their music. It has a certain sound, melody, harmony, rhythm, instrumentation, language and subject matter that speaks to the hearts of those people. It is a direct application of the words of Jesus, "From the abundance of the heart the mouth speaks."

If the worship team is leading only one generation, things are simple. When more than one generation wants to worship, things get more complicated. They also get more interesting and much more fun musically.

Cultural Elements of Worship are Temporary

Like a worship service itself, cultural worship elements will come and go. They are important because through them we lead people in the worship of the Lord. We must realize that despite our affection for or disgust of the cultural elements of worship, they are doomed to pass away with time. Consider the Psalms of the great King David. We have only the slightest idea of what his music sounded like. It has passed from the scene to be replaced by the music of every generation of those who sang the psalms. The words remain and this is the lesson we must all learn if we are to lead the whole church in worship—see what will pass and see what will remain.

> **1 Thessalonians 5:19-21**
> Quench not the Spirit. Despise not prophesyings. Prove all things; hold fast that which is good.

Time and the Worship Service

In addition to unfolding within time with a beginning a middle and an end, a worship service should feature three dimensions of time:

Past (Thanksgiving—honoring what God has done)

Present (Worship—encountering the Lord Jesus today) and

Future (Prayer—preparing for the coming days).

There will be more about this later.

WORSHIP IS ROOTED IN ETERNITY

While worship leading is experienced in time, worship itself is rooted in the eternal. If worship leading is the study of changing things, worship is the study of unchanging things. In fact, worship has its essence in the very character of God, the holy, complete, changeless, character of God. The worship theme of the Old Covenant is heard so many times in the Old Testament. It is some variation of this confession: "The Lord is good and His mercy endures forever!" Jesus based His instructions on prayer on the character of the Father. "Don't pray like pagans! Your Father knows your needs!" The constancy of God's character is the centerpiece of heaven. Thus, the song of the angels, "Holy, Holy, Holy!"

Throne Room Worship

The Throne of God and of the Lamb lies at the heart of worship study. Here is both our example and our reality. Eternally, without ceasing, the hosts of heaven worship God. We see this in the book of Revelation. The book of Hebrews informs us that this includes a gallery of the faithful who have preceded us to heaven.[1] In Isaiah and Revelation we have the texts of the worship songs used by these hosts:[2]

- "Holy, holy, holy, is the LORD of hosts: the whole earth is full of his glory."

- "Holy, holy, holy, Lord God Almighty, which was, and is, and is to come."

- "Thou art worthy, O Lord, to receive glory and honor and power: for thou hast created all things, and for thy pleasure they are and were created."

- "Worthy is the Lamb that was slain to receive power, and riches, and wisdom, and strength, and honor, and glory, and blessing."

- "Blessing, and honor, and glory, and power, be unto him that sitteth upon the throne, and unto the Lamb for ever and ever."

These songs are truly eternal; they never cease. Each new generation of worship songwriters sets these timeless words in their own musical styles. Why? Because when we worship God here on earth, we are actually joining the constant worship of heaven. What a privilege!

The Heavenly Pattern

How do we get from earth to glory? There is a "new and living way" opened by Jesus![3] When God gave Israel a movable

---

1   Hebrews 12:22-24
2   Isaiah 6:3 Revelation 4 and 5
3   Hebrews 10:19-25

sanctuary in the wilderness, it was designed after the pattern of
the Throne Room of God. Moses was given strict instructions
not to vary from the pattern he saw in heaven.[1] Thus Moses'
Tabernacle is the template for worship for all time. It was not just
for that ancient wilderness trek; it is for us today. This pattern
shows us how to come before the Lord. Through Jesus, it is the
"new and living way."

Then and Now

The Tabernacle and the Temple were shadows or likenesses
of the Throne Room of God in heaven. Now, under the New
Covenant, we actually enter the heavenly tabernacle when we
worship in Spirit and Truth! When we study the Tabernacle /
Temple model we will see this in greater detail.

CONCLUSION
A TIME OF SHAKING

Hebrews 12:27-29

And this word, Yet once more, signifieth the removing of
those things that are shaken, as of things that are made, that
those things which cannot be shaken may remain. Wherefore
we receiving a kingdom which cannot be moved, let us have
grace, whereby we may serve God acceptably with reverence
and godly fear: for our God is a consuming fire.

The study of worship is a detailed biblical exposition of
eternal things. The highly effective worship team recognizes
this. The time-bound things will come and go but these things
are constant. We must see the difference. If we do not, we
face the danger of confusing the two. We may dispose of the
indispensable and hold fast to the disposable.

Postmodern life is a time of shaking. The Lord is doing the
shaking so the eternal things which cannot be shaken can be

---

1   Hebrews 8:5

clearly seen. Let us test all things and hold fast to the eternal things while letting the temporary things function for their time and then let them go.

DISCUSSION QUESTIONS

1. Explain the concept of polarities.

2. What does this statement mean: Worship happens at the intersection of time and eternity.

3. What are some polarities in Jesus' teaching?

4. What is the concept of the dynamic center?

5. What is the relationship between worship and culture?

6. Explain the concept of the heart-song.

7. How is worship on earth connected to the worship in heaven?

In Time and in Eternity, Worship is More than Music!

Chapter Three

FINDING a BIBLICAL VOCABULARY

> **Psalm 19:14**
> Let the words of my mouth, and the meditation of my heart,
> be acceptable in thy sight,
> O Lord, my strength, and my redeemer.

INTRODUCTION

The Importance of Words

Language is a precious gift from God. As such it must be carefully used and constantly protected from misuse. Language is so important the Incarnation is spoken of as words as seen in John's description:

> **John 1:1**
> In the beginning was the Word,
> and the Word was with God, and the Word was God.

> **John 1:14**
> And the Word was made flesh, and dwelt among us, (and we beheld his glory, the glory as of the only begotten of the Father,) full of grace and truth.

Words play vital roles in our lives.

- Words matter to God; His Word is communicated through words.
- Words matter to us; our worship is communicated with words.
- Words are the doorways to the mind and heart.
- Words are the connectors to the hearts of others.

Checking our Worship Vocabulary

Each worship leader and team member uses a worship vocabulary. We have nouns, verbs, adjectives, and adverbs that help us communicate with each other. We also have holy words, straight from the Bible that express the joy and longing in our hearts for communion with God. In this chapter we will seek out a worship vocabulary from the Word of God itself, one based in eternity, standing above the temporary terminology of today's fleeting cultures.

It is important that we obtain a biblical vocabulary because the concepts behind the words also have cultural terminologies. These, like all cultural entities, are rooted in time and will have temporary use. We can use them within their cultural origin but it is more helpful to also have in our possession their biblical counterparts. These are the eternal things that empower the temporary things. These are the truths we must transfer to the next generation. To discover the biblical terms, we must rely on standard dictionaries of the original languages of scripture.

SPIRIT AND TRUTH WORSHIP

At the heart of a biblical worship vocabulary lies the pivotal truth Jesus gave us in His conversation with the Woman at the Samaritan Well.

> ### John 4:23-24
> But the hour cometh, and now is, when the true worshippers shall worship the Father in spirit and in truth: for the Father seeketh such to worship him. God is a Spirit: and they that worship him must worship him in spirit and in truth.

Sometimes the original languages reveal hidden meanings that are lost or altered when translated into English. This is not the case here. The Greek words for spirit and truth mean the same as the English words. How do we determine their meaning to us?

- "Spirit" has to do with invisible things in life— breathing—air put to purpose—the breath of life. We get so many invisible but vital things from "spirit:" inspiration, respiration, expiration, and so forth.
- "Truth" just means—"truth,"—something that is valid, not false.

How do these apply to the worship the Father is seeking?

- To worship in spirit means to worship from the inner, invisible self, the totality of our human being.
- To worship in truth means to worship sincerely, according to valid facts and revelations and with no false motives.

Let's apply these meanings to worship.

- To worship in spirit means to worship as directed and empowered by the Holy Spirit.
- To worship in truth means to worship according to the truth of God.

Let's put these things together to solidify our understanding of worship in spirit and truth:

- To worship in spirit means to worship from our spirit as led and empowered by God's Spirit.
- To worship in truth means to worship with our truth according to God's truth.

This is True Worship and the Father is looking for people who will offer Him this kind of worship.

Exploring these Polarities

The division of worship into these polarities is observable in many ways. These observations can help us understand the things we see in worship today.

- There are "spirit people" who prefer emotional, exciting, constantly new worship.
- There are "truth people" who prefer intellectual, low-key, comfortably traditional worship. The Father is looking for people who will stretch beyond their comfort zones to worship Him.
- There are "spirit songs" which do not engage the mind but allow the emotions to soar. These tend to be choruses without many words and few if any verses.
- There are "truth songs" which greatly engage the mind and require rapt attention and the ability to concentrate. These tend to be songs with verses and choruses and other parts with many words.

The constant interplay between spirit and truth is at the heart of the energy of True Worship.

Praise and Worship

Fundamental to worship and worship leading is the difference between praise and worship. Sometimes these words are used interchangeably but they are not synonyms. There are many Hebrew words for praise and worship. We will deal with two Greek words to achieve a biblical understanding: *doxa-* meaning glory and *proskuneo* meaning to prostrate oneself.

Here are two verses where these words are used.

Ephesians 1:12
...that we who first trusted in Christ
should be to the praise of His glory (doxa).

Matthew 28:9
And as they went to tell his disciples,
behold, Jesus met them, saying, All hail. And they came and
held him by the feet, and worshiped him. (proskuneo)

Common uses of the English words help us understand the difference between these two words.

- Praise - to express a favorable judgment of: to commend.[1]
- Worship - to honor or reverence as a divine being or supernatural power.[2]

We can and should praise people and things. It is altogether proper that we should praise those who do well or to commend an item or event as excellent and praiseworthy. We must never worship people or things. It is not proper for us to worship individuals, events, or items. The word worship is derived from an Old English term, "worth-ship," denoting a supreme state of worthiness. This state of worthiness is reserved for God only. This is why idolatry is such a serious sin. It is profane to ascribe the worthiness of God to some object or individual! The first of the Ten Commandments covers this and is reinforced by the words of Jesus that loving and worshiping God is the highest and greatest duty of mankind.

The Praise-to-Worship Sequence

The distinctions between praise and worship clear up the mystery of how worship should flow in the worship service: Praise precedes worship.

---

1 Merriam-Webster
2 Merriam-Webster

- Praise is an act of obedience. We praise God because He is worthy and because we are commanded to do it. It has nothing to do with how we feel.

- As an act of the will, praise is seated in the mind and body. We consider the worthiness of God and we decide to give Him praise. This is done by the action of the body: standing, singing, lifting hands, etc.

- Worship is a response of the human spirit to the revelation of God. This goes deeper than praise. Our spirits bear witness with the Holy Spirit that we are in relationship with God; we are His children.

Romans 8:14-16

For as many as are led by the Spirit of God, they are the sons of God. For ye have not received the spirit of bondage again to fear; but ye have received the Spirit of adoption, whereby we cry, Abba, Father. The Spirit itself beareth witness with our spirit, that we are the children of God.

The Praise-to-worship sequence recognizes this. Worship is a response to revelation so revelation must precede worship. This revelation can come from two sources:

1. the Word of God that prompts or informs our worship

2. the manifestation of the presence of God.

Let us consider the most important passage in the Old Testament to the understanding of worship: Psalm 22:3 We need to check it in both the KJV and the NKJV

Psalm 22:3

But thou art holy, O thou that inhabitest the praises of Israel.
KJV

But You are holy, Enthroned in the praises of Israel. NKJV

God Responds to the Praises of His People!

This is an attribute of God. He responds to the praises of His people! He is always faithful to respond in two specific ways:

1. with His holy presence and
2. with His marvelous sovereignty.

He inhabits and is enthroned upon our praise. This attribute of God's character explains the praise-to-worship sequence.

- We begin with praise and proceed to worship. We begin with our physical and mental obedience to the call of God to worship and the revelation of His worthiness.
- He then responds with His manifest presence and we respond to His presence with worship from our spirits.

This is why services often begin with lively songs and proceed to slower songs. Of course, praise is not limited to fast songs nor is worship limited to slow ones. What is really at work is the praise-leads-to-worship sequence seen in so many passages of scripture.[1]

The Praise-to-Worship Sequence in Scripture

Praise	Worship
Ps 24:3 Who may ascend into the hill of the LORD?	Or who may stand in His holy place?
Ps 29: 1-2 Give unto the LORD, O ye mighty, give unto the LORD glory and strength. Give unto the LORD the glory due unto his name;	worship the LORD in the beauty of holiness.
Ps 99: 5 Exalt the LORD our God,	And worship at His footstool — He *is* holy
Ps 99:9 Exalt the LORD our God,	And worship at His holy hill; For the LORD our God *is* holy.
James 4:8 Draw nigh to God	and he will draw nigh to you.

The Praise-to-Worship sequence is illustrated in the Wilderness Tabernacle and is the template for worship as it occurs in heaven as we will see when we discover the Seven Biblical Models for worship.

---

1   Psalms 24:3; 29:1-2,99:1-2, 9; James 4:8

Psalms, Hymns and Spiritual Songs

Some of the most important biblical words to understand are these: "Psalms, hymns, and spiritual songs." There are so many cultural names for song types that confusion results if we do not see the eternal behind the cultural. These three types of songs are mentioned in two places in the Bible, once in relation to the Spirit and the other in relation to the truth of Christ.

Ephesians 5:18-20

And be not drunk with wine, wherein is excess; but be filled with the Spirit; Speaking to yourselves in psalms and hymns and spiritual songs, singing and making melody in your heart to the Lord; Giving thanks always for all things unto God and the Father in the name of our Lord Jesus Christ;

Colossians 3:16

Let the word of Christ dwell in you richly in all wisdom; teaching and admonishing one another in psalms and hymns and spiritual songs, singing with grace in your hearts to the Lord.

Here are the biblical meanings from Vine's Dictionary of NT words: **Psalm**—"a sacred song, sung to musical accompaniment" **Hymn**—"a song of praise addressed to God" **Spiritual Song**—always connotes the ideas of invisibility and of power. It does not occur in the Sept. nor in the Gospels; it is, in fact, an after-Pentecost word. ...spiritual songs are songs of which the burden is the things revealed by the Spirit..."

- Psalms are songs of praise with instrumental accompaniment, either from the Psalm or of recent composition.

- Hymns are not songs in books, or old songs, or traditional songs; they are songs of prayer.

- Spiritual Songs are songs sung within the move of the Spirit. This type of song was new to the New Covenant and involved content as the Spirit gave utterance.

When we judge the music we use in worship, we should look for these three types of songs:

1. Songs of praise with instruments,

2. Songs of prayer, and

3. Songs of the Spirit.

CONCLUSION

Biblical Ideals

We do not live in biblical times and we should not try to replicate those ancient departed cultures. What we must do is learn the eternal things spoken of in the Bible and use our cultural languages and practices in biblical ways. If we are to become a highly effective worship team, we should understand and pursue Spirit and Truth. We should function within the blessings of a complete understanding of Praise and Worship. We should compose, perform, and enjoy all three types of songs mentioned in the Bible.

DISCUSSION QUESTIONS

1. Discuss the importance of words in worship, in life.

2. Discuss the "spirit" aspects of worship, the "truth" aspects.

3. What are some examples of "spirit songs?" "Truth songs?"

4. What are the unique aspects of praise? Of Worship?

5. What are your observations of the Praise-to-Worship sequence?

6. Discuss Romans 8:14-16.

7. Discuss the different functions of psalms, hymns, and spiritual songs.

Even with Psalms, Hymns, and Spiritual Songs, Worship is More than Music!

Chapter Four

GOD'S DWELLING PLACES

Biblical Models 1 and 2

> **Psalm 100:2**
> Serve the Lord with gladness:
> come before his presence with singing.

INTRODUCTION

Understanding the Presence of God

Sometimes people ask: How do we come into the presence of a God who is everywhere? In the Bible we see three dimensions of God's presence:

1. God's Omnipresence—He is everywhere [1]

2. God's Covenantal or Inner Presence in the Hearts of His People[2], and

3. God's Manifest Presence in the praises of His People[3].

In simpler language we can express it this way:

- God is.
- God is with us.
- God is moving among us.

---

1   Psalm 139:7-12
2   2 Corinthians 6:14-18
3   Psalm 22:3

Jesus told Nicodemus that the Holy Spirit was like the wind, unseen but powerful in its effect[1].

The manifest presence of the Lord is exactly like this.

* The Omnipresence of the Lord is like the atmosphere, unseen but essential to life.
* His Inner Presence is like the oxygen in our blood giving us life from the inmost parts to our extremities.
* God's Manifest Presence is like the wind. When air moves we become aware of it. A gentle breeze refreshes. A mighty wind impresses. Perhaps this is why old time Pentecostals and other Evangelicals spoke of a great worship service or a revival as "a move of God."

The role of the worship team is to come into the service filled with the Omnipresence of God, empowered by the Inner presence of God to go with the people of God into the Manifest Presence of God.

Altars

Before the Lord commanded that dwelling places be built for Him to inhabit, those who sought His presence built altars of sacrifice. This is still the basis of all true worship, a sacrifice unto the Lord. Repentance on our part, offered in humility invites the forgiveness of God which He is ready to provide. When the sin barrier is removed, we enter into fellowship with God. This is what the human heart longs for; this is the need of the human soul and the crying desire of the human spirit. This is what the human race lost in Eden and what we regain in True Worship. It happens at the altar.

The Patriarchs

Before Moses received the plans for the Tabernacle, the great heroes of the faith built altars of sacrifice to meet with God.

* Noah carried extra sacrificial animals on the Ark for the purposes of worshiping God after the flood.[2]

---

1   John 3:8
2   Genesis 8:20

- Abraham built three altars.[1]
- Isaac[2] and Jacob followed his example.[3]

In later centuries, The Tabernacle in the Wilderness and the Temple of Solomon were designed around altars of sacrifice.

- The Brazen Altar in the Outer Court,
- The Altar of Incense in the Holy Place, and
- The Mercy Seat in the Holy of Holies.

In response to the sacrifices of worshipers, God met with them at these altars.

Moses

With the deliverance of Israel from Egypt, the People of God needed more than makeshift altars. They needed for the Manifest Presence of God to dwell visibly in their midst. They needed it and God wanted it. He missed the joys of Eden as well! God loves to dwell in the midst of His people! He loves to inhabit our praise! That is why it is fitting for the upright to praise Him![4]

Moses' Tabernacle in the Wilderness was a portable system of tents placed at the center of the nation.

- **The Holy of Holies.** At the heart of the Tabernacle was the Holy of Holies, the Most Holy Place, where the Ark of the Covenant was kept secure behind a heavy curtain called, "The Veil." Only the High Priest could enter the Holy of Holies and he only once a year to make a sacrifice for the sins of the nation. The Shekinah, the supernatural glow of the manifest presence of God, rested on the Ark.

- **The Holy Place.** Preceding this Holy of Holies was another tented room called the Holy Place. It contained

---

1 Genesis 12:7; 13:4; 22:9
2 Genesis 26:25
3 Genesis 33:20; 35:1,3
4 Psalm 33:1

three pieces of furniture: The Altar of Incense, The Table of Bread, and The Golden Lampstand. These were regularly tended by holy priests.

- **The Outer Court.** The entire system of tents was surrounded by tent-like walls enclosing the Outer Court. Here personal sacrifices for sin were made. There was a brass altar where the sacrifice was killed and a brass bowl, called "the sea," where the priests could wash their hands.
- **The Beautiful Gate.** The Tabernacle area was entered through an elaborately decorated Gate. The walls of the Tabernacle were of drab sand-colored fabric but the Gate of Thanksgiving, a type of Jesus, was colorful and beautifully decorated.
- **The Shekinah Glory.** Over the Ark and the Tabernacle was the visible manifestation of the Presence of God: a pillar of fire by night and a pillar of smoke by day. When the visible presence and the Ark moved the people broke camp and moved with it.

King Solomon

Generations later, after the Promised Land had been occupied and made secure, King David's son, Solomon was privileged to build a permanent structure to house the worship of the people and the Manifest Presence of God. We call it Solomon's temple.

The Glory of the Lord filled both of these structures when they were dedicated: The Tabernacle of Moses[1] and the Temple of Solomon[2]. Several generations later when the People of God broke covenant with Jehovah for the final time, invaders destroyed Solomon's Temple and took the finest of the people captive to foreign lands. After a number of years, reformers rose up and the leaders returned from captivity and built another Temple, called Zerubbabel's Temple, a smaller, less elaborate structure to be sure, but Covenantal worship was reestablished. [3]

1 Exodus 40:34-38
2 II Chronicles 5:11-14
3 Ezra 6:16

King David

Between Moses' Tabernacle and Solomon's Temple, the Ark rested and worship happened at a tent on Mount Zion in Jerusalem called the Tabernacle of David. Here's the story of how this tabernacle came about.

David wanted with all his heart to build a house for the Lord but that was not God's plan for him. One of the great achievements of David's reign was the restoration of the Ark of the Covenant which had been captured by the Philistines. King Saul had shone no interest in the Ark and the Philistines had found it too dangerous to keep. (This is one of the great OT stories that every worship leader should study.) When David had become king in both the north and the south he attempted to bring up the Ark. His first attempt failed because he used his own methods rather than those prescribed by Scripture—a lesson for us all. His second attempt, done according to the plan of God, was successful. David placed the Ark in a tent on Mt. Zion and established a new order of musical priests. This House of God was quite different from Moses' Tabernacle, which, torn, tattered, and old, was still in use with an empty Holy of Holies.[1] How was David's Tabernacle different?

- The Ark of the Covenant was available to all.

- The principle sacrifice was the Sacrifice of Praise.

- All the worship arts mentioned in the Psalms began here.

- Everyone could come to the Ark and worship God.

This was the beginning of corporate worship and the Book of Psalms.

---

1 There is no record that the Ark of the Covenant was ever returned to the Tabernacle of Mosea. Psalm 78, a teaching piece relating the whole history of Israel, states that God rejected the Old Tabernacle and chose David and Mt. Zion Psalm 78:67-72.

MODELS FOR THE UNDERSTANDING OF WORSHIP

These historical realities serve us today as models for the understanding of worship. These two structures, the Tabernacle/ Temple and David's Tabernacle, serve as illustrations of worship in spirit and truth—New Covenant worship. These are called "types" and they are fulfilled in Christ.

The Tabernacle /Temple Model

The Book of Hebrews informs us that on Mt. Sinai Moses saw the throne of God in heaven.[1] He was told to design the Tabernacle in its shape. Why? Because worship is the act of coming before the presence of God. We actually join the worship going on in Heaven, in Zion above. The Tabernacle in the Wilderness was more than a provisional blessing to get the nation through the desert and into the Promised Land. It was a copy of God's Throne Room in Heaven—the heavenly Zion. This pattern continues to this day. This is why worship services start with thanksgiving and joy and end with altar time; this is the pattern of Heaven! A worship service is a progression through the Tabernacle/Temple Model:

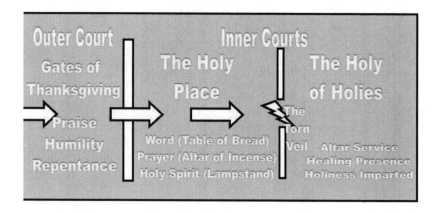

---

1 Hebrews 8:5

Hebrews 8:5

Who serve unto the example and shadow of heavenly things,
as Moses was admonished of God when he was about to make
the tabernacle: for, See, saith he, that thou make all things
according to the pattern shewed to thee in the mount.

Hebrews 12:22-24

But ye are come unto mount Zion, and unto the city of the
living God, the heavenly Jerusalem, and to an innumerable
company of angels, To the general assembly and church of the
firstborn, which are written in heaven, and to God the Judge
of all, and to the spirits of just men made perfect, And to
Jesus the mediator of the new covenant, and to the blood of
sprinkling, that speaketh better things than that of Abel.

The Tabernacle/Temple Model is the template for New Covenant worship.

Model No.1
The Tabernacle/Temple
OUTER COURT

Gates of Thanksgiving — For who He is and what He has done
Courts of Praise — Exaltation of His name and character
Altar of Sacrifice — Repentance, humility, offerings

INNER COURT
The Holy Place

Altar of Incense — Effectual Prayers of Petition/Intercession
Table of Bread — Public Reading, Preaching the Word
The Golden Lampstand — Light and Power of the Holy Spirit

The Holy of Holies

The Ark of the Covenant — God's Manifest Presence

David's Tabernacle Model

The Tabernacle of David also conforms to the pattern of heaven in that we begin with praise and proceed to worship. It is best expressed in Psalm 24:

Psalm 24:3-10
Who shall ascend into the hill of the Lord? or who shall stand in his holy place? He that hath clean hands, and a pure heart; who hath not lifted up his soul unto vanity, nor sworn deceitfully. He shall receive the blessing from the Lord, and righteousness from the God of his salvation. This is the generation of them that seek him, that seek thy face, O Jacob. Selah. Lift up your heads, O ye gates; and be ye lifted up, ye everlasting doors; and the King of glory shall come in. Who is this King of glory? The Lord strong and mighty, the Lord mighty in battle. Lift up your heads, O ye gates; even lift them up, ye everlasting doors; and the King of glory shall come in. Who is this King of glory? The Lord of hosts, he is the King of glory. Selah.

The fundamental question is, "Who shall truly worship God?"

- Who shall ascend the Hill of the Lord? In other words, "Who shall praise the Lord?"

- Who shall stand in the Holy Place? In other words, "Who shall worship?"

Praise is the action of the will and worship is the response of the spirit.

The answer is, "He who has clean hands, a pure heart"—these are only obtained by way of the Cross—and he who has kept his heart and life pure—these things come from the power of the Holy Spirit. What is the result of this pattern? "The King of Glory" comes into the room!

David's Tabernacle is a prophetic portrait of the New Testament church. How is this like the church?

- Corporate, all-inclusive worship for "Whosoever Will."
- The Primary Sacrifice is the Sacrifice of Praise.
- Singers, instrumentalists, and the worship arts are used.

The Biblical Study of the Tabernacle of David

For a greater understanding of this model, follow this stream of Biblical witness.

Tabernacle of David

Psalm 78:67-72	God abandoned Old Tabernacle; Chooses David and Mt. Zion
Isaiah 16:5	Messiah will sit and judge from the Tabernacle of David.
Amos 9:11,12	God will rebuild the Tabernacle of David so that all of mankind can see the Lord.
Acts 15:17-22	James quotes Amos to end the Acts 15 conference and open the Gospel to all people.
Hebrews 12:19-24	When the NT church worships, we go to Mount Zion!

Model No. 2
David's Tabernacle
Worship as desrcibed in Psalms
WORSHIP ORDER: PSALM 24:3

"Ascend the Hill of the Lord" ——————————— PRAISE!

"Come before His presence with joyful songs" (Ps 100:2)
"Give thanks" (Ps 18:49)
"Celebrate!"(Ps 145:7)

"Stand in the Holy Place" ——————————— WORSHIP!

"Worship and bow down" (Ps 95:6)
"Receive the Word of God" (Ps 19:7-14)
"Wait on God" (Ps 62:1)
"Pray" (Ps 61:1-2)
"Seek God's Face" (Ps 24:6)

CONCLUSION

These great historical structures functioned in their day as the dwelling places of God under the Old Covenant. Today, under the New Covenant, they serve as Biblical Models for the study of worship. In the Tabernacle/Temple model, we find the protocol of heaven. The highly effective worship team never forgets this.

DISCUSSION QUESTIONS

1. Why are biblical models needed for worship today?

2. Why do we turn to the Old Testament to understand New Testament Worship?

3. Discuss the three dimensions of the presence of God.

4. How does the heavenly protocol of the Tabernacle/Temple Model relate to the Praise-leads-to–worship sequence?

5. Does Almighty God still desire a dwelling place in the midst of His People? If so, where is that dwelling place?

6. What are some of the Worship Arts called for in the Book of Psalms?

7. How do the promises found in Psalm 22:3 relate to these biblical models?

When We Ascend the Hill of the Lord and Stand in the Holy Place We Know that Worship is More than Music!

Chapter Five

OUR IDENTITY and FUNCTION

Biblical Models 3 and 4

---

1 Peter 2:5,9

Ye also, as lively stones, are built up a spiritual house, an holy priesthood, to offer up spiritual sacrifices, acceptable to God by Jesus Christ…. But ye are a chosen generation, a royal priesthood, an holy nation, a peculiar people; that ye should shew forth the praises of him who hath called you out of darkness into his marvelous light…

Hebrews 13:15-16

By him therefore let us offer the sacrifice of praise to God continually, that is, the fruit of our lips giving thanks to his name. But to do good and to communicate forget not: for with such sacrifices God is well pleased.

Romans 12:1

I beseech you therefore, brethren, by the mercies of God, that ye present your bodies a living sacrifice, holy, acceptable unto God, which is your reasonable service.

INTRODUCTION

Our Identity and Function as Worshipers

In addition to the identification cards, passwords, and numbers we all carry around in our wallets, purses, or brains, each of us also carries a special identity in the Lord. We are Holy-Royal Priests unto the Lord. Along with the jobs we may hold, the skills we may possess, and passions we may pursue, each of us also has a special function to perform for the Lord. We minister to the Lord with the Living Sacrifice of Praise. Whether or not we are conscious of it, all worshipers of the Lord Jesus possess this important identity and this special function. Biblical Models 3 and 4 describe these things.

The Biblical View

All people have an inner vision of who they are and what they are supposed to do. Until the will of God comes into focus, people, worship team members, in particular, will have inner visions based on temporary, not eternal things. This is another polarity.

Both the temporary self-understanding and the eternal one are true at the same time. While we are singers, players, leaders, followers, craftsmen, technicians, and administrators on the worship team, we are at the same time Holy-Royal Priests unto the Lord. As we function on the team singing, playing, leading, following, working our craft, operating our tech or overseeing the whole business, we are really ministering to the Lord with the Living-Sacrifice of Praise. Our primary, biblical, and eternal identity and function gives meaning and purpose to the temporary job assignment. This truth equalizes team members, making us all equally important to the Lord.

Model No. 3

THE HOLY-ROYAL PRIESTHOOD

This idea is not some leadership mind game; this is right out of the Bible! The Apostle Peter informs us.

---

1 Peter 2:5,9

Ye also, as lively stones, are built up a spiritual house, an holy priesthood, to offer up spiritual sacrifices, acceptable to God by Jesus Christ.... But ye are a chosen generation, a royal priesthood, an holy nation, a peculiar people; that ye should shew forth the praises of him who hath called you out of darkness into his marvelous light...

The New Testament Priesthood

To understand what St. Peter is telling us we need to erase the images of other types of priests from our minds. He is not talking about Roman Catholic priests or those from Eastern religions or jungle cults. He is talking about the Priesthood of the Old Covenant. The Old Testament priesthood is a type of the New Testament priesthood. Peter announces two descriptive terms:

1. holy, and
2. royal.

These are not synonyms. The distinctions between them are important.

We are Holy Priests

New Covenant worshipers are a Holy Priesthood, set apart for the ministry of worship — "to offer up spiritual sacrifices acceptable to God through Jesus Christ."[1] There is no way to overemphasize the importance of these words. They describe who we are and what we do.

- We have been made holy by the Blood of Jesus. We offer more than songs; we minister to the Lord with the Living Sacrifice of Praise.

- We have been set apart—sanctified, anointed, chosen, *empowered*—to worship God in Spirit and in Truth, to give unto Him the glory due His name.[2] We do this in private worship, in public worship, and in our private and public lives.

To understand how we do this, we need to understand that from the beginning, at least as far back as the smoking heights of Mt. Sinai, God had intended that His People would be a kingdom of priests.

From the Mountaintop to the Valley Below

The Lord warned Moses, high in the mountain, that things were not going well in the valley below. Before he reached the foot of Mt. Sinai, the sound of "worship" reached his ears. He held in his hands the tablets of stone that would call for worship with detailed instructions on how it should be done and what it would mean. Soon the tablets would crash to the ground and break.

Who was leading the worship at the foot of the mountain? How was it being done? The answers to these questions would break Moses' heart and anger Almighty God. Up there in the mountain, Moses interceded for the people so recently ascended from Egyptian slavery. In the valley, Aaron, the brother of Moses, fashioned in gold a calf and the people were "worshiping" with all of their might.

1   I Peter 2:5
2   Psalm 29:1-2

The wrath of God burned through Moses and a worship purge left thousands dead and focused the nation on true worship—worship by the Book. The orgy of "worship" also wrought a change, a delay really, in the plan of God for mankind. Read the Lord's words at the giving of the Law and sense his plan for the world.

> **Exodus 19:6a**
> And ye shall be unto me a kingdom of priests,
> and an holy nation.

Yet, after the worship of the golden calf, the Lord selected the sons of Aaron and tribe of Levi to be a priestly tribe.

> **Exodus 29:44-46**
> And I will sanctify the tabernacle of the congregation, and the altar: I will sanctify also both Aaron and his sons, to minister to me in the priest's office. And I will dwell among the children of Israel, and will be their God. And they shall know that I am the Lord their God, that brought them forth out of the land of Egypt, that I may dwell among them: I am the Lord their God.
> **Numbers 1:50**
> But thou shalt appoint the Levites over the tabernacle of testimony, and over all the vessels thereof, and over all things that belong to it: they shall bear the tabernacle, and all the vessels thereof; and they shall minister unto it, and shall encamp round about the tabernacle.

The terrible disobedience of people and the spineless "leadership" of Aaron postponed the plan of God all the way from the giving of the Law at Mt Sinai to the giving of his Son at Mt. Calvary. What God intended at Mt. Sinai, He has accomplished at Mt. Calvary. The Apostle Peter makes it clear. John's revelation shines a universal light on this Calvary-cleansed kingdom/ priesthood.

> **Revelation 5:9-10**
> And they sung a new song, saying,
> Thou art worthy to take the book, and to open the seals
> thereof: for thou wast slain, and hast redeemed us to God by
> thy blood out of every kindred, and tongue, and people, and
> nation; And hast made us unto our God kings and priests:
> and we shall reign on the earth.

This is the New Testament Church!

The church has been raised up out of the Egypt of sin to be the Holy Nation, the Kingdom of priests, the Holy-Royal Priesthood. We have a vital ministry to perform to the Lord Himself—True Worship. And we have a ministry to the world—telling them the Jesus Story. Under the old covenant the priests had responsibilities in three broad areas:

1. worship and worship leading,

2. learning and teaching the Word of God, and

3. assisting in the processes of redemption.

These are also the areas of ministry for the new covenant priests.

Royal Priests unto the Lord Worship God with Heart, Soul, Mind, and Strength.

Individually, we are each a holy, royal priest unto the Lord. This truth frames and fuels our private worship. When we gather to worship, we form the holy, royal priesthood. Without this theology of public worship, the focus of each event quickly moves to us:

- the songs we like,

- the ceremonies we prefer,

- the preaching that blesses us,

- the prayers that reinforce our comfort zones.

How transforming it would be if our worship leaders and rank and file worshipers would see themselves as priests unto the Lord, a Kingdom of Priests.

- Jesus would be the focus of every service.
- The Holy Spirit would have a free hand to move among us.
- The Lord Jesus would rule over us granting miracles and deliverances, signs and wonders, saving the lost, restoring the weak, healing the sick and calling people to lives of service.

Called to a life of intimacy with God Himself and charged with the assignment of communicating and living out the Word of God, the Holy Royal Priesthood is a force for good in the world. As priests unto the Lord, we tell the Jesus Story to the world. We do this as we worship, as we preach, as we witness, and, most importantly as we *live.*

Model No.3
The Holy-Royal Priesthood
Illustrates our relationship with God

We are Holy Priests

We carry the Ark of His Presence. (1 Pt 2:4-5, 1 Ch 15:2)
We minister to the Lord. (1 Ch 16:4-6)
We offer spiritual sacrifices. (1 Pt 2:4-5)
Our personal worth is based on His love, not our achievement. (Dt 7:7-8)

We are Royal Priests

We are called to be with Him. (Mk 3:13; 1 Pt 2:9)
We are called to be His friend. (Jn 15:12-17)
We are a chosen generation (family line) (1 Pt 2)
We are a holy nation, a purchased people to proclaim his excellence. (1 Pt 2)

Model No. 4

THE LIVING SACRIFICE OF PRAISE

An Aroma Pleasing to the Lord.

Every evening, every morning, throughout the centuries of Old Testament worship, the smoke of sacrifices coiled upward from the Tabernacle and later from the Temple. Every year the man of Israel, the priest of his home, would select from his flock the finest male lamb to offer to the Lord as a sacrifice on the Day of Atonement. Since it was the man's sins that required atonement, under the guidance of the priest, the man would slay the lamb himself.

When the instructions for offering these sacrifices to the Lord are given in Leviticus a strange statement is made repeatedly.

> **Leviticus 1:9**
> the priest shall burn all on the altar, to be a burnt sacrifice, an offering made by fire, of a sweet savour unto the Lord.

Modern translations say this is an aroma pleasing to the Lord. Does our God enjoy the smell of burning flesh and hair, of grain and oil? Since God is *spirit*[1] the smells of the material world, so unavoidable to us, do not register in his awareness as they do in ours. What was the *spiritual aroma* that pleased him when an Old Testament worshiper put the knife to the lamb or lifted the grain and waved before the Lord?

Jesus made it clear that true worship emanates from the heart; to worship the Father who is *spirit,* we must enter the realm of the *Spirit* and do so in truth. The New Testament sacrifice is the sacrifice of praise. It is putting the knife to our own pride and self-reliance.

1   John 4:24

Worship is a sacrifice.

The fundamental biblical image of worship is that of the sacrifice. In the Old Testament, the record is clear. From Eden to the Kingdom of Israel only the sacrifice of blood could bring worshipers closer to God. King David serves as an example. He was chosen to be king in Saul's place because his heart was right. Later in life, David refused to offer a sacrifice on ground given to him with these words:

---

2 Samuel 24:24
And the king said unto Araunah,
Nay; but I will surely buy it of thee at a price: neither will I offer burnt offerings unto the Lord my God of that which doth cost me nothing. So David bought the threshing floor and the oxen for fifty shekels of silver.

In the New Testament, Mary of Bethany offered to Jesus a costly sacrifice of praise when she lavished her most prized possession on the Lord. She won His highest commendations. He also connected the preaching of the undiluted Word of God with this costly sacrifice of praise.

Matthew 26:10, 12
Why trouble ye the woman?
for she hath wrought a good work upon me.

("She has done a beautiful thing to me." ESV)
For in that she hath poured this ointment on my body,
she did it for my burial.

Mark 14:8-9
She hath done what she could: Verily I say unto you,
Wheresoever this gospel shall be preached throughout the whole world, this also that she hath done shall be spoken of for a memorial of her.

The Bible says Mary's tribute began to prepare His body for the ordeal ahead. The meaning of Jesus' death is that of the final sacrificial lamb. His is not the story of a young man tragically struck down by society; it is the story of a willing, perfect sacrifice. The writer to the Hebrews explains that, like the material veil torn in the Temple at the moment of His death, Jesus' body was the spiritual veil torn to open the way for a fallen mankind to enter the presence of a Holy God.[1] Paul exalted this costly sacrifice as the example for us in worship.

> **Philippians 2:5-8**
> Let this mind be in you, which was also in Christ Jesus:
> Who, being in the form of God, thought it not robbery to be
> equal with God: But made himself of no reputation, and took
> upon him the form of a servant, and was made in the likeness
> of men: And being found in fashion as a man, he humbled
> himself, and became obedient unto death,
> even the death of the cross.

The aroma God loves is the spiritual scent of hearts being emptied before Him, the self-inflicted wounding of our human pride. As the Psalmist said,

> **Psalm 51:17**
> The sacrifices of God are a broken spirit: a broken and a
> contrite heart, O God, thou wilt not despise.

The Living Sacrifice of Praise is both an event and a process.

The Living Sacrifice of Praise

Event & Process

---

1 Hebrews 10:19-25

The Event:

Paul, in his letter to the Romans, presents powerful promises to the one who would offer his humanity to the Lord as a living sacrifice.

> **Romans 12:1-2**
> I beseech you therefore, brethren, by the mercies of God, that ye present your bodies a living sacrifice, holy, acceptable unto God, which is your reasonable service. And be not conformed to this world: but be ye transformed by the renewing of your mind, that ye may prove what is that good, and acceptable, and perfect, will of God.

What are those promises?

- The destructive patterns of life in a fallen world will be broken.

- The worshiper's mind will be renewed and he will prove the fullness of God's will.

Somehow this meager presentation of our fallen, wounded selves, this voluntary lifting up of our hearts, hands, and voices to Him in worship, is pleasing to God. Surely this is the "aroma pleasing to the Lord." No wonder Paul pleads with the Romans to enter into this sacrifice of praise. It is a reasonable thing to do.

The Process:

The writer to the Hebrews exalts the Sacrifice of Praise to the pinnacle of his exposition of the New Covenant.

> **Hebrews 13:15-16**
> By him therefore let us offer the sacrifice of praise to God continually, that is, the fruit of our lips giving thanks to his name. But to do good and to communicate forget not: for with such sacrifices God is well pleased.

This is more than the event described in Romans 12; this is
a continual offering, a life-process like breathing. The attitude of
praise (gratitude, humility) should be as consistent as respiration,
a constant intake of heaven's atmosphere into our earthbound
spirits. This will result in the fruit of our lips confessing His
name and the fruit of our lives as we "do good and to share
with others, for with such sacrifices God is pleased." This is the
"aroma pleasing to the Lord."

> ## Model No.4
> ### The Living Sacrifice of Praise
> #### Illustrates our Ministry to God
> ## The Living Sacrifice
> The Event: the presentation of the body (Ro 12:1-2)
> (attendance to worship, hands, voice, etc.)
> The reasonable service of worship, (praise-to-worship sequence)
> Renews the mind, breaks the world's mold, proves the will of God
> ## The Sacrifice of Praise
> The Process: The Continual Ministry (He 13:15-16)
> (finds expression in all aspects of life)
> Vocal Praise: The fruit of lips than confess His name. (He 13)
> Do good and share with others (deeds of mercy, words of witness)

CONCLUSION

Worship Team ministry becomes more joyful and more
manageable when we realize who we are in God. We are not
mechanics and nurses, teachers and executives—we are Holy-
Royal Priests. We are made holy by His blood and made Royal
by His decree and call. We do not just make music, we minister
to the Lord with the Living sacrifice of Praise! How wonderful
when our earthly lives unfolding in time, find eternal significance
in the plan of God!

DISCUSSION QUESTIONS

1. Why did God abandon His plan for the nation of Israel to be a Kingdom of Priests?

2. What does it mean to be God's Holy Priest?

3. What does it mean to be God's Royal Priest?

4. What does it mean to "minister to the Lord with the Sacrifice of Praise?"

5. In what ways do we "present our bodies" to the Lord?

6. What are the differences between the "event" of the Sacrifice of Praise and the "process" of the Sacrifice of Praise?

7. Discuss the promised effect of the presentation of the Living Sacrifice of Praise in Romans 12:1-2.

As Priests unto the Lord, We Know that Worship Is More than Music!

Chapter Six

THE DIVINE RESPONSE

Biblical Models 5, 6, and 7

> **Psalm 22:3-5**
> But thou art holy, O thou that inhabitest the praises of Israel.
> Our fathers trusted in thee: they trusted, and thou didst
> deliver them. They cried unto thee, and were delivered: they
> trusted in thee, and were not confounded.

INTRODUCTION

BEFORE THE THRONE OF GOD— ENTERING THE REALM OF THE SOVEREIGNTY OF GOD

Extending the Kingdom of God

The Psalmist declares, "The earth is the Lord's..." He invites us to "Lift up your heads, O you gates! And be lifted up, you everlasting doors!" He promises, "And the King of glory shall come in."[1] Because the Lord is enthroned upon the praises of His people, when we worship God the King does indeed "come in!" We sense His presence, that wonderful God-moment when anything might happen. The entrance of

1 Psalm 24

the King into our midst is the goal of every worship service. In truth, we extend the Kingdom of God into our time and space by humbling ourselves before Him in praise and worship. The Lord responds to the humble heart with the wonderful gift of His presence, His sovereignty come to earth. In the words of the writer to the Hebrews, "We have come to Mt. Zion!"[1] What is it like in the throne room of Heaven? The Bible gives us two detailed visions of the Throne of God and a three-point definition of what the Kingdom of God is in substance.

Model No. 5

THE THRONE OF GOD AND OF THE LAMB

What Is It Like Before the Throne of God?

Looking to Isaiah chapter six and the Book of Revelation we see what the Throne Room of God is like.

Biblical Visions of God's Throne Room	
Isaiah's Vision: (Isaiah 6)	John's Vision: (Revelation 4-5)
A Majestic Throne	A Majestic Throne
All focus was on the One	All focus was on the One
The sounds of Worship: "Holy, Holy, Holy" "Worthy Is the Lamb"	The sounds of Worship: "Holy, Holy, Holy"
Isaiah struck with awe	John struck with awe
God was obeyed.	God was obeyed.

The throne room of heaven is a place where God is worshiped continually by angels and creatures, elders, and saints. The focus is on the One-Who-Sits-on-the-Throne. The will of God gets done here. There is no rebellion, no self-centeredness, no straying minds or wandering eyes. Jesus is the center of all. There is unity of spirit and purpose although men and women are there from every tribe and tongue and nation. Jesus has made them into one whole, worshiping family. There is continual

1   Hebrews 12:22-24

music and confession, ceremony, and liturgy. And there is visual beauty beyond the mind of man to comprehend.

This brief description, inspired by the reports of Isaiah and John, reveals how off-centered and impoverished our worship can become. When the desires of man are at the center, we design worship to imitate the world not to mirror heaven. With proud hearts on display and rebellious spirits in command, only lip service is paid to the will of God. How far we have drifted from the Throne of God!

The Sovereignty of God

But we have His promise. He *will* be enthroned upon our praise! If we humble our hearts and turn to Him and begin to invest our worship with the liturgy of heaven, *He will receive our worship to be His Throne!* We can know the joy and power of His sovereignty among us, "His kingdom, come and His will done" among us, here and now. Paul gives us the test of our worship in his definition of the Kingdom of God.

> ### Romans 14:17
> For the kingdom of God is not meat and drink; but righteousness, and peace, and joy in the Holy Ghost.

When we can look at the church and see these three characteristics at work (righteousness, peace and joy in the Holy Spirit) then our worship is actually an extension of the Kingdom of God. But if there is hidden sin, unrest, and strife, or depression and discouragement, then some other king has come. His will is being done, not the Lord's.

Beholding His Glory

At the Throne of God, lives are changed. When we enter the realm of the splendor of His majesty and sovereignty, miracles, signs, and wonders happen. Worshipers, like the prophet Isaiah, hear the call of the God to service. If we wonder why we have a dearth of miracles, signs, and wonders and why so few are hearing the call of God into a life of service, perhaps this is part of the answer. These things happen at the Throne of God.

If we wonder why there is a dearth of character in the church, we must consider how far we are from the Throne of God. Paul said to behold the glory of the Lord was to be changed, just as Isaiah and John were never the same after their visions of the Throne of God.

---

2 Corinthians 3:18

But we all, with open face beholding as in a glass the glory of the Lord, are changed into the same image from glory to glory, even as by the Spirit of the Lord.

Lord, show us Your glory so that we might be changed!

Model No.5

The Throne of God
God's Response to Praise and Worship

Psalm 22:3
God takes our praise to be His Dwelling and Ruling Place (Mt. Zion)

Isaiah 6:1-8/Revelation 4-5
The Throne Room of God Is a place of:

Praise and Worship   Awe and Wonder
The Revelation of God   Submission to God
Service to God

Romans 14:17

The Kingdom Is Righteousness, Peace, Joy

Model No. 6

THE OFFICE PLACE OF THE LORD

> **Acts 13:1-3**
>
> Now there were in the church that was at Antioch certain prophets and teachers; as Barnabas, and Simeon that was called Niger, and Lucius of Cyrene, and Manaen, which had been brought up with Herod the tetrarch, and Saul. As they ministered to the Lord, and fasted, the Holy Ghost said, Separate me Barnabas and Saul for the work whereunto I have called them. And when they had fasted and prayed, and laid their hands on them, they sent them away.

Ministry to the Lord

This biblical phrase, "minister to the Lord" is an absolute key to the understanding of worship. The NIV translates this as "worshiped the Lord" and that is a good translation. The Greek word is *leitourgeo,* meaning "to be a public servant, ... (by analogy) to perform religious or charitable functions (worship, obey, relieve): KJV - minister."[1]

Another resource gives the word this definition: *leitourgeo*, in classical Greek, signified at Athens "to supply public offices at one's own cost, to render public service to the State"; hence, generally, "to do service," said, e.g., of service to the gods. In the NT ... it is used (a) of the prophets and teachers in the church at Antioch, who "ministered to the Lord,"[2]

At Antioch, this spiritual leaders were in fasting and worshiping the Lord, probably in a liturgical style like the worship in the Temple since this same word is used to describe that kind of worship in Hebrews 10:11. In fact, this Greek word is the source of the English word, "liturgy." The literal meaning of the word *leitourgeo*—to provide the Lord a place to do His work—is an exciting concept of worship.

---

1   Vine's Dictionary of New Testament Words
2   Strong's Concordance

The Office-Place of the Lord

The idea is simple enough: when we worship in Spirit and Truth, we provide the Lord with an earthly place to do His work.

- When we truly worship Him, our sanctuaries become His Office-place.

- Our lives, our workstations, our homes, every capacity of life that is given over the Lord as praise and worship can be a place for Him to do His work in the world.

The Ministry of the Messiah

What is the Lord's work? It is the ministry of the Messiah as prophesied by Isaiah and claimed by Jesus.[1]

Luke 4:18-19

The Spirit of the Lord is upon me, because he hath anointed me to preach the gospel to the poor; he hath sent me to heal the brokenhearted, to preach deliverance to the captives, and recovering of sight to the blind, to set at liberty them that are bruised, To preach the acceptable year of the Lord.

This is still His work today. When we minister to Him, He ministers through us.

- The Holy Spirit makes Jesus real as we tell His story in worship.

- He embraces those who worship Him.

- He sets people free as we worship Him.

- Those who are spiritually blind see clearly as the Spirit ministers Christ to them.

- Those who are oppressed, bruised by the enemy of their souls with shackles that cruelly bind, are set at liberty by His power as we go about living for Him, following His call, seeking His anointing, telling His story, worshiping Him with heart, soul, mind, and strength.

---

1 Isaiah 61; Luke 4

Worshipers are healers in this world. Our words can be His words, our touch His touch, our embrace His loving caress. Worshiping churches are healing stations in this world, hospitals of the wounded heart. There is a work that only Jesus can do but He has chosen to do it through His people. The Lord Jesus wants to set up His office in your life and mine, in your church and mine. Let us be faithful to minister to the Lord.

Model No. 6
The Office-place of the Lord
Healing and Restoration through Worship

Acts 13:2

When we worship the Lord, our worship becomes His office-place.

Luke 4:18-19
The Lord's Office Work is:

To preach the Gospel to the poor,
To heal the broken hearted,
To preach deliverance to the captives,
The recovery of sight to the blind,
To set at liberty those who are bruised, and
To preach the acceptable year of the Lord.

Model No. 7

THE RIVER OF LIFE

While there are many references to the river of God's blessings, two detailed descriptions, one from the Old Testament and the other from the New Testament are striking in their similarity and powerful in their promise.

Ezekiel 47:1-12

Then he brought me back to the door of the temple; and there was water, flowing from under the threshold of the house…And when the man went out to the east with the line in his hand, he measured one thousand cubits, and he brought me through the waters; the water came up to my ankles. Again he measured one thousand and brought me through the waters; the water came up to my knees. Again he measured one thousand and brought me through; the water came up to my waist. Again he measured one thousand, and it was a river that I could not cross; for the water was too deep, water in which one must swim, a river that could not be crossed. He said to me, "Son of man, have you seen this?" Then he brought me and returned me to the bank of the river. When I returned, there, along the bank of the river, were very many trees on one side and the other. Then he said to me: "This water flows toward the eastern region, goes down into the valley, and enters the sea. When it reaches the sea, its waters are healed. And it shall be that every living thing that moves, wherever the rivers go, will live. … everything will live wherever the river goes…But its swamps and marshes will not be healed; they will be given over to salt.

Revelation 22:1-5

And he showed me a pure river of water of life, clear as crystal, proceeding from the throne of God and of the Lamb. In the middle of its street, and on either side of the river, was the tree of life, which bore twelve fruits, each tree yielding its fruit every month. The leaves of the tree were for the healing of the nations. And there shall be no more curse, but the throne of God and of the Lamb shall be in it, and His servants shall serve Him. They shall see His face, and His name shall be on their foreheads.

The River of Life is a Healing Stream

One of the most vivid images of the power of worship is the River of Life, seen in Ezekiel 47 and Revelation 22, two strikingly parallel passages. Other references include the Psalms[1] and the words of Jesus[2]. In Ezekiel's vision, we see four depths to the river: ankle deep, knee deep, waist deep and waters over the head. Ezekiel and his angel-guide passed through the first three levels but found the fourth depth too large to cross. It was a river in which one must swim. I observe four levels in our worship experience: thanksgiving, proclamation, adoration, and communion. These correspond to the four depths of the river in Ezekiel's vision.

Ankle-Deep (Thanksgiving) Is Refreshing.

We enter the ankle-deep waters of life when we give thanksgiving to the Lord. Psalm 100 identifies thanksgiving as the gateway to the presence of the Lord. Like standing ankle deep in a stream, thanksgiving is refreshing to the soul. But this is a level intended as a passage, not for a dwelling place, so we must go out deeper.

Knee-Deep (Proclamation) Is Impressive

When we are standing knee-deep in a river, we can feel the current. In fact, we have to counter the force of the river with every step. When we go beyond thanksgiving and begin to proclaim the Lord's excellence, His character, deeds, and love, we also move from refreshing to a state of being impressed with the Lord's power. Thanksgiving and praise refresh and impress us with God's power, but these are levels of expression through which we must pass.

Waist-Deep (Adoration) Is Life-Altering

When we move from knee-deep to waist-deep in the waters of life, we are going from the proclamation of praise to the expression of adoration. We have moved from praise to worship,

---

1   Psalms 1; 36, 46
2   John 7:38

from speaking about God to speaking to Him, from an emphasis on what He has done for us to who He is in us. At this point, change begins to happen. Entering the Lord's presence with thanksgiving and praise does not bring about lasting change. We can exit the river at the exact spot we entered. The next passage to waters that are waist-deep, begins the process of being altered by the waters. The river carries us downstream with every step.

This explains why churches can be active in praise but still not progress toward the holiness the Lord expects from them. Praise is refreshing and impressive but it is not transforming. Paul said that to contemplate his glory was to be changed. When we begin to worship the Lord, we begin to be changed. This takes time; time we are sometimes reluctant to allot to corporate worship. For decades this time was found in those wonderful, long altar services in the American Pentecostal tradition, in camp meetings in the Great Awakenings, and in extended revivals spawned by those Great Awakenings that impacted Evangelical churches.

Waters-over-the-Head Is Transformational

Still, this incredible privilege of standing waist-deep in the waters of life is also a passageway and not a destination. Ezekiel's angel-guide brought him out another thousand steps. At this point, Ezekiel had to swim, to let go and launch himself into the presence of the Lord. The first result was that he got wet all over. Many of us know what this is in worship, to be immersed in the presence of the Lord. These experiences change us forever. This is the place where

- baptism in the Spirit happens,
- calls to the ministry are heard,
- miracles and healings take place,
- bondages are broken and
- shackles of sin are destroyed.

This level of spirit-deep communion with God is still available to us in the secret place and in the public place. The river still flows in its fullness from the Throne of God and of the Lamb.

Beware the Shallow Places

In Ezekiel's vision, the shallow marshes were not healed. His words are stark: "But its swamps and marshes will not be healed; they will be given over to salt."[1] We should be wary of shallow, me-centered, time-conscious worship. The Spirit is calling us out deeper into the waters of life That's where the healing is, not in the stagnant backwaters of culture.

What does this mean to the Worship Team?

It means that when we are worshiping God and leading others in worship, the Holy Spirit is flowing like a River of Life through us. The River flows from the Throne of God in our hearts. The Holy Spirit, the life of God, flows through our worship just as the River Jordan flowed from the Sea of Galilee. The Jordan River flows and waters the whole nation of Israel on its way to the Dead Sea, one of the lowest spots on earth.

In Ezekiel's prophetic vision, he sees the River of Life flowing from the Throne of God in Heaven and all the way to the Dead Sea of human need. When the waters of life touch the barren sea, the waters are healed and new life begins. The prophet makes a powerful promise:

Ezekiel 47:9 NKJV
And it shall be that every living thing that moves, wherever the rivers go, will live.

This is the flow of the life of God! It is powerful and restorative in its effect. This is what happens when the church

---

1 Ezekiel 47:11 But the miry places thereof and the marshes thereof shall not be healed; they shall be given to salt.

worships God: the Waters of Life flow into broken, hopeless lives and they are healed. Let us enter the flow with praise and dwell there in worship! We will see God change lives!

Model No. 7
The River of Life
Entering the Flow of the Holy Spirit

ILLUSTRATION	REALITY
(Ezekiel 47:1-11)	(Revelation 22:1-5)
Water flowing from the Throne in the Temple	The Holy Spirit flows from the Throne of God.
Passed through ankle-deep water	Thanksgiving (the gateway to His Presence)
Passed through knee-deep water	Praise/Exaltation (the proclamation of His character
Passed through waist-deep water	Worship/Adoration (commitment to God)
Cannot pass through waters-over-the-head; had to swim; A river that cannot be crossed.	Communion with God (revelation of God)
The River flows to the Dead Sea	The Spirit flows toward human need.
The Dead Sea comes to life!	Human need is met by Jesus!

Wherever the River goes everything will live.

CONCLUSION

Our brief biblical study of worship concludes with the Seven Biblical Models for the Understanding of Worship. This is only an introduction to the subject. I invite you to read my book, *Worship that Pleases God—The Passion and Reason of True Worship.* You'll find it at Amazon in both paperback, Kindle, and digital versions. Also, if you have questions concerning biblical concepts and current issues in worship log on to my Worship Renewal Center website, StevePhifer.com for a complete library of articles on worship, worship leading, and Christian artistry.

DISCUSSION QUESTIONS

1. Discuss the concept of coming before the Throne of God when we worship.

2. Discuss the three-fold description of the Kingdom of God: righteousness, peace, and joy—in the Holy Spirit.

3. How does True Worship supply an Office-place for the Lord?

4. What are some of the ministries of the Lord in His Office-place?

5. Discuss the four levels in Ezekiel's River and how they relate to the worship service.

6. How is the flow of the Holy Spirit like the flow of a mighty river?

7. Discuss the impact of a worshiping church on this hurting world.

As Life Flows from the Throne of God, We Know that Worship Is More than Music!

THE SEVEN BIBLICAL MODELS
OF WORSHIP

-Moses' Tabernacle
-David's Tabernacle

-The Holy-Royal
   Priesthood
-The Living Sacrfice
   of Praise

-The Throne of God
-The Lord's Office
-The River of Life

the
worshiprenewal center
stevephifer.com
semper reformanda

Part Two:

PART TWO
WORSHIP LEADING

Psalm 57:7 ESV
My heart is steadfast, O God, my heart is steadfast! I will sing and make melody!

Psalm 29:1-2
Give unto the LORD, O ye mighty, give unto the LORD glory and strength. Give unto the LORD the glory due unto his name; worship the LORD in the beauty of holiness.

Ephesians 5:18-21

And be not drunk with wine, wherein is excess; but be filled with the Spirit; Speaking to yourselves in psalms and hymns and spiritual songs, singing and making melody in your heart to the Lord; Giving thanks always for all things unto God and the Father in the name of our Lord Jesus Christ; Submitting yourselves one to another in the fear of God.

Colossians 3:16-17

Let the word of Christ dwell in you richly in all wisdom; teaching and admonishing one another in psalms and hymns and spiritual songs, singing with grace in your hearts to the Lord. And whatsoever ye do in word or deed, do all in the name of the Lord Jesus, giving thanks to God and the Father by him.

Chapter Seven

THE LEADERSHIP of the Spirit

INTRODUCTION

Spirit to Spirit

> **Romans 8:14-17**
> For as many as are led by the Spirit of God, these are sons of God. For you did not receive the spirit of bondage again to fear, but you received the Spirit of adoption by whom we cry out, "Abba, Father." The Spirit Himself bears witness with our spirit that we are children of God, and if children, then heirs — heirs of God and joint heirs with Christ, if indeed we suffer with Him, that we may also be glorified together.

Abba Father

The fundamental heart-cry of worship is "Abba, Father!" Deep in the spirit of the worship team member the voice of the Holy Spirit witnesses to the excellence and nearness of God. The human spirit responds to this call with worship. What does this mean? It means that all the utterances of praise and worship are expressions of a relationship. They are responses to the revelation of who God, our Father, is. We are the children of God! A spirit-to-Spirit connection is made and expressed in songs, confessions, and sacred actions.

- The light of the Holy Spirit reveals the majesty of God to us.
- The fire of the Holy Spirit purifies us.
- The oil of the Holy Spirit heals us.
- The strength of the Holy Spirit empowers us.

This connection also extends outward to our brothers and sisters around us in the worship space. There is a bond between worshipers that is strong and beneficial both to those on the team and those in the congregation.

The Father's Quest

Jesus said the Father was looking for True Worshipers, those who would worship Him in spirit and truth. This is the fundamental polarity of worship.

This is not a choice between these two forces but a powerful synthesis of the two. This is what the Father is looking for from His church. We have spent 6 chapters exploring the truth on worship—and there is still so much more to learn! In this chapter we will take a close look at how the Spirit of God leads us in worship.

THE ABIDING SPIRIT

From the Old Covenant to the New

The relationship between worshipers and the Holy Spirit changed with the New Covenant. Under the Old Covenant, the

Holy Spirit came on people to empower them for a specific task and then lifted from them. Under the New Covenant, the Holy Spirit abides within the redeemed spirit of the worshiper, a permanent source of blessing. Jesus made this clear at the Last Supper.

John 14:15-18

- The Holy Spirit is called the Comforter or Helper: The world cannot receive the Spirit.
- Under the Old Covenant, the Spirit was *with* worshipers but not *in* them.
- Under the New Covenant, the Spirit abides within the worshiper.
- Jesus comes to us through the ministry of the Holy Spirit.

John 14:25-26

- The Holy Spirit teaches us all things.
- He reminds us of the Word of God.

John 15:26

- He is called the Spirit of Truth.
- He testifies of Jesus.

John 16:7-11; 12-15

- The Holy Spirit convicts the world of sin, righteousness, and judgment to come.
- The Spirit guides us in all truth.
- He speaks of things to come.
- He speaks with the authority of Jesus.
- He glorifies Jesus.

It is easy to see why worship teams need to be well acquainted with the ministry of the Holy Spirit. The result of true redemption is the abiding presence of the Holy Spirit in our lives. The ministry of the Holy Spirit is to exalt Jesus, an essential factor in the ministry of the worship team.

The Anointing of the Holy Spirit

We often hear talk about the anointing of the Holy Spirit. Many times this talk is done in mysterious tones as if this were a mystery only a few can understand. It is really quite simple:

1. The anointing is a sign of God's choice.

2. The anointing is the flow of God's power.

There is no mystery here; just simple observation of scriptural examples. This is another worship polarity: Skill and Anointing.

God's Choice.

Under the Old Covenant, leaders were anointed with a special mixture of oils used only for this purpose. This marked the individual for a particular life of service to God. Objects like the furnishings of the Tabernacle and Temple were also anointed, set apart for the worship of God. In the New Testament, the Greek word for anointing refers to the setting apart of a person for service to the Lord.

God's Power.

It makes sense that when God chooses someone that He also empowers them. The great example of this is the story of Aaron's tribal rod. In a time of challenge to the leadership of Moses and Aaron, the Lord devised a test to prove whom He had chosen to lead the nation. The head of each of the 12 tribes put his rod, a walking stick and the symbol of his power, in the Tent of Meeting overnight. The next morning, eleven of the rods were unchanged but Aaron's rod had budded and produced almonds! The flow of God's power proved God's choice of Aaron. This is still true today; the flow of the power of the Spirit proves one's anointing.

The Anointing Today

Each Christ-follower has an anointing, a ministry to which God has called him or her. How does one know what his/her anointing might be? There are some simple tests:

1. Do you have a sense that God has called you to this?
2. Do you have an interest in the skills required by this calling?
3. When you fulfill this calling, do the results go beyond your skills?
4. Does your ministry in this area bless others and bring you joy?
5. Does it point to Jesus?

The secret of a great worship team is having people ministering in the area of their anointing. That's when the power of the Holy Spirit can flow at the greatest strength.

The anointing is the partner of skill. There was a time when church people thought that one could either be skilled or anointed but not both. Not true! God intends that anointed people gain the skills required to do what they are called to do. To understand this, consider this passage of Scripture:

---
2 Corinthians 4:7
But we have this treasure in earthen vessels, that the excellency of the power may be of God, and not of us.

What does this mean to us today?

- We are the earthen vessel—a human being, with talents and skills.

- The treasure is the Holy Spirit—the power of God.

Our humanity shapes the work of the Holy Spirit in us, the way liquid in a jar takes on the shape of the jar. For example:

- Instrumentalists can only play in the keys they have mastered.

- Singers can only sing in the range they have, and so on.

Deeper than our humanity, the power of the Holy Spirit — truly a treasure!— enables us to minister beyond the limits of our skill. Skill resides in our soul and body while the anointing abides in our spirit. Ministry results from human skill amplified by divine power. This understanding of the anointing of the Holy Spirit inspires us to discover our anointing, develop the necessary skills, and prayerfully depend on God to use us for His glory.

The Partnership of Skill and Anointing

Touching People

Talents and Skills reside in the human soul and body.

Touching God

The Abiding Spirit of God in the human spirit.

Spirit-Empowered Ministry

Touching God   Touching People

The Baptism with the Spirit

John the Baptist prophesied this about Jesus:

Mark 1:8

I indeed have baptized you with water: but he shall baptize
you with the Holy Ghost.

It happened on the Day of Pentecost as recorded in the
second chapter of Acts.

Acts 2:1-4

When the Day of Pentecost had fully come, they were all with
one accord in one place. And suddenly there came a sound
from heaven, as of a rushing mighty wind, and it filled the
whole house where they were sitting. Then there appeared
to them divided tongues, as of fire, and one sat upon each of
them. And they were all filled with the Holy Spirit and began
to speak with other tongues, as the Spirit gave them utterance.

The rest of the story in the book of Acts is the account of
how Christ-followers who were thus immersed in the power of
the Spirit carried the Gospel to their world. This understanding
of Spirit-Baptism was lost and found through the various epochs
of church history and experienced a rebirth at the beginning of
the 20th Century in what is known as the Pentecostal Revival. In
the last three decades of that century, the charismatic renewal
extended Spirit-Baptism into mainline churches. Today this
spirituality is an accepted branch of Christian orthodoxy in
Protestant, Roman Catholic, and Eastern Orthodox circles. What
is this Spirit-Baptism promised by John and received by the 120
at Pentecost?

The image of immersion in water is an effective picture of
what it is like to receive Spirit-baptism. The Baptism with the
Spirit is: an immersion into the power and presence of Jesus in
which Jesus releases the Holy Spirit into our lives who brings
about:

- The initiation of the prayer language, that is, praying in
  tongues,

- The introduction to the Gifts of the Spirit for worship and ministry purposes,
- The endowment of spiritual power for service, and
- The intensification of the direct leadership of the Holy Spirit in daily living.

This is the new norm! The full power of the Apostolic life is available through the abiding ministry of the Holy Spirit. In the arena of prayer, the fullness of the Spirit has a most profound impact on life and ministry. First Century Prayer Paradigm has been restored.

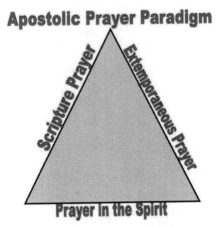

We will go deeper into the Apostolic Prayer Paradigm in Chapter Eleven.

WORSHIP IN THE SPIRIT

All these centuries later, the words of Jesus to the woman at the Samaritan well still guide us in our choices about how we should worship in spirit and in truth. When the church gathers to worship, the impact of the Holy Spirit on the individual worshiper is multiplied in powerful ways. In the Sermon on the Mount Jesus said each of us is like a candle shining in the darkness. When we are all in the same place at the same time, our individual lights combine and we become a shining City on a Hill that cannot be hidden.

> ### Matthew 5:14-16
> Ye are the light of the world. A city that is set on an hill
> cannot be hid. Neither do men light a candle, and put it
> under a bushel, but on a candlestick; and it giveth light unto
> all that are in the house. Let your light so shine before men,
> that they may see your good works,
> and glorify your Father which is in heaven.

This is the power of worship in spirit and truth! We become a witness to the glory of the Lord and a testimony to those who do not know the Lord—a Shining City on a Hill! The Spirit helps us worship. He helps us pray, give thanks, proclaim praise, and remember the Scriptures in the service itself. He also helps us plan, prepares us to lead, and then assists us while we are leading.

The Spirit also convicts the lost. This is His job, not ours! Our job is to exalt the Lord Jesus and then the Holy Spirit takes it from there. The same song that exalts the Lord will edify the believer and convict the sinner next to him/her! It is the exaltation of Christ that does the work of the ministry.

The Ways of the Spirit of God

It is vital that the goals of the worship leader, the lead worshiper, and the worship team members be aligned with the goals of the Holy Spirit. We cannot expect God to bless us and use us if our goals are different from His. How do we determine what the goals of the Holy Spirit are in each service? The answers are found in the Scriptures. There are two types of passages that instruct us in these matters:

1. Directives tell us what to do. These come from direct commands and from the historical accounts of worshipers who pleased God.

2. Principles guide us in our leadership choices. These are drawn from the purposes of God implicit in the scriptural record.

Directives are many and varied and are often contradictory to each other. The Bible tells to shout and to be silent, to move and to be still, to weep and to rejoice and so forth. How do we know when to do what? The principles guide us in knowing when to do what.

The Three Principles of the Holy Spirit in Worship

Careful attention to the words of Jesus at the Last Supper and the instructions of Paul to the Corinthian church reveal three principles that are always true in a worship service.

1. The Holy Spirit moves to exalt Jesus.[1]
2. The Holy Spirit moves to edify the church.[2]
3. The Holy Spirit moves decently and in order.[3]

These three things are always true. Sometimes we are led to shout and sometimes to be silent but always in a way that exalts Jesus, edifies the church, and moves decently and in order. The same is true for any of the other worship directives.

These goals are also the tests of what we do in worship. When considering a song or a ceremony or an event within a service we must ask:

1. Does this exalt Jesus?
2. Does it edify the whole church?
3. Does it unfold in a fitting and orderly way?

With the addition of the direct leadership of the Holy Spirit prompting us to plan this thing for our service, we can be sure that we have found the mind of Christ.

CONCLUSION

This understanding of the role of the Holy Spirit in our lives has much to say to the worship team member. These are our responsibilities:

---

1   John 14-16
2   I Corinthians 14: 26
3   I Corinthians 14:40

- We must seek to understand and function within our anointing.

- We must examine our hearts as we seek to align our purposes with those of the Holy Spirit.

To do this we can ask the same questions of our heart that we ask of elements of a worship service:

- Is my heart's goal to exalt the Lord Jesus?

- It my chief aim to edify the church?

- Do I do my best to flow as the Spirit flows, decently and in order?

- The answers to these questions are personal but the effect of them is visible by all with eyes to see.

A Highly Functional Worship Team is one that is dependent upon the anointing of the Holy Spirit.

DISCUSSION QUESTIONS

1. Discuss the importance of the phrase "Abba Father" and its relation to the Holy Spirit.

2. What is the difference between the Old Covenant and New Covenant ministries of the   Holy Spirit?

3. What are the two aspects of the anointing of the Holy Spirit?

4. Discuss the partnership of skill and anointing.

5. What did John the Baptist mean when he promised that Jesus would baptize believers—with the Holy Spirit and with fire?

6. What are the three modes of prayer under the New Covenant?

7. Discuss the three goals of the Holy Spirit in the worship service.

With the Ministry of the Holy Spirit,
Worship Is More than Music!

Chapter Eight

THE HEART of the TRUE WORSHIPER

| **Matthew 12:35** |
| A good man out of the good treasure of the heart bringeth forth good things... |

| **Psalm 57:7 ESV** |
| My heart is steadfast, O God, my heart is steadfast! I will sing and make melody! |

INTRODUCTION

THE ARTS AND WORSHIP

A public worship service is a work of public art. When worship is expressed, it is expressed through the arts.

- We compose impromptu praises and prayers.

- We recite scriptures and the prayers others have written.

- We sing songs of our own and those written by others.

- Instrumentalists play their instruments for the glory of God.

- Preachers research and prepare, fashioning public addresses on the glory and story of God.

- Congregations sing together—public art at the highest level.

Art is the product of the heart of the artist. Jesus said that from the abundance of the heart the mouth speaks. This is true of everyone and it is especially true for members of the worship team. If we want our music making and technical support efforts to be pure before the people, our hearts have to be made pure before the Lord first. This is a ministry of the Holy Spirit.

Lazarus—a Type of the Reborn Artist

When Jesus raised the brother of Mary and Martha of Bethany from the dead what He did not do is significant. He brought Lazarus back from the dead and out of the tomb, but He did not remove the grave clothes from him. He told his friends to do that: "Loose him and let him go."[1]

It is the job of the worship arts pastor to take worship team members and "loose them and let them go!" In other words, worship team member, the condition of your heart is the ministry of your worship leader! Why? Because the arts of worship are sometimes learned in the world, not in the church. When salvation comes and with it a call to do worship ministry, team members trained in the world may still be wearing the grave clothes! We may have learned our skills in the wrong context and we need to relearn them in the context of the Kingdom of God. The worship pastor must:

- Unwrap the eyes and provide a newer, brighter vision,
- Unwrap the head for newer, better concepts and content,
- Unbind the heart to feel new and better passions,
- Loosen the lungs to breathe the free air of the Spirit,
- Untie the hands for new levels of service to the Lord, and
- Release the feet to walk a new, life-long path of service.

In the world, skill matters most; in the Kingdom of God, heart matters the most.

1   John 11:44

- Pride is the cornerstone of music education; In the Kingdom of God. pride is replaced by integrity and diligence. Humility is the essence of worship; pride is the antithesis of worship.

- Stardom is the goal of the entertainment world; service is the coin of the realm in the Kingdom of God.

- Externals determine worth in the world; internals are the most important thing in the Kingdom of God.

For those of us who were trained in the systems of this world, there is work to be done. We must unlearn the wrong things and re-envision our talents and skills in the light of the Anointing of the Holy Spirit. Outward things are important, but they must be real, not an act or even a job. Here we see another polarity:

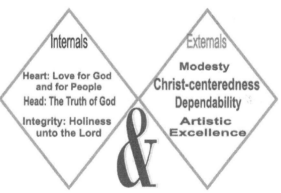

The powerful truth is this: The internals will produce the externals, good or bad. This is both a warning and an opportunity. When the congregation sees the ministry of the worship team we want them to see modesty, Christ-centeredness, dependability, and artistic excellence. These things are outward witnesses of these inward realities: love for God and for people, the truth of God, and above all, a pure heart.

A TALE OF HEARTS

The Bible tells an impressive set of stories centered around the hearts of a series of leaders:

Hannah[1] was the mother of the prophet/judge Samuel. She was one of two wives. Her husband's other wife had produced children but Hannah was barren. Her heart would not let her accept an unacceptable situation so she went to the Tabernacle to pray for a child. The High Priest, Eli, thought she was a prostitute and accused her of drunkenness. When she told him the real story, he blessed her and proclaimed that God had heard her prayer. He had and soon she brought her son, Samuel, and gave him to the priest to raise. Thus began the career of a mighty man of God—all because of a woman's heart who believed God for an impossible blessing.

Samuel[2] was the last judge of Israel and the one who anointed the first two kings. As a child, he learned the value of ministering to the Lord. He was without fear of men and was totally dedicated to God. He anointed Saul and denounced him when his heart led him to false worship. Samuel had a heart that feared God and not men.

Saul[3] was anointed to be king by the hand of Samuel, quite against Samuel's will. The nation wanted to be like other nations and have a king. It was not yet God's time and Samuel knew this but did as he was told. The heart of Saul was not the heart of a king, so God gave him a new one.[4] At that moment a group of prophets came singing and playing instruments on the way to the Tabernacle. When they came near Saul, the Spirit of the Lord came on him and he began to prophesy. His new heart made Saul into a different man and all could see this difference. But Saul did not continue to develop this new heart and it was replaced by a cold, self-centered, political heart that cost him his kingdom.

David[5] is described as a man "after God's own heart."[6] The story of his anointing and ascent to the throne lies at the

---

1   1 Samuel 1 and 2
2   1 and 2 Samuel 1 Samuel
3   1 Chronicles
4   1 Samuel 10:9-11
5   Samuel 1 and 2
6   Acts 13:22

heart of the history of Israel and should be a major study for each worship team member. For our purposes here, let us look at this description, a man "after God's own heart." It means two powerful things. First, the heart of David looked like the heart of God. We will explore this when we look at the heart of Jesus. Secondly, the word "after" also means "to pursue." David was a man who pursued the heart of God. When his heart failed him and no longer reflected the heart of God, as in his adultery with Bathsheba, David continued to pursue the heart of God with repentance. He wanted nothing more than for God to dwell in the center of his own life and in the center of the nation.

Jesus[1] told his disciples that when they had seen Him they had seen the Father. Jesus is the revelation of God to mankind. Here we see the reflection of the heart of King David in the heart of King Jesus! Their hearts were full of the Word of God. They each had hearts for prayer early in the day. They loved righteousness and were broken hearted over sin—David over his own sins and Jesus over ours.

Lessons Learned from this Tale of Hearts

We need not accept the unacceptable! Like Hannah, we can take our impossibilities to the Lord in prayer and in faith and see things change! If we have a heart to please the Lord like Samuel, we can be fearless in what God has called us to do because we are ministering to Him! If we have heart problems like Saul, God can give us a new heart and show us how to maintain it. We can be a person "after the heart of God" in both likeness of His great heart and in the pursuit of His heart.

The Heart of God Is Revealed in Jesus

Pursuing the Heart of God

This is the job of every worship team member—to pursue the heart of God. Each of us should strive to be a person, "after the Heart of God." Repeated exposure to the Holy Spirit in

---

1   Matthew, Mark, Luke, John, Acts, Revelation

private prayer and public worship gives the Lord opportunity to change us to be more like Jesus. This common goal in the heart of each team member is the glue that holds the team together. Like a standard pitch we all try to match when preparing to play, the common desire to be like Christ gives the team a shared goal. When one of us falls short of this goal, the others can understand and pray for us and encourage us, not judge us. So what is the heart of Jesus like?

- The heart of Jesus is a holy heart; there is only good, no wickedness at all.
- The heart of Jesus is a humble heart; He routinely shunned power over others.
- The heart of Jesus is a responsible heart; while He shunned power, He welcomed responsibility.
- The heart of Jesus is a courageous heart; we too can be brave for Him.
- The heart of Jesus is a compassionate heart; "They will know we are Christians by our love."
- The heart of Jesus is a passionate heart; we too can love God and our neighbors.

From the Abundance of the Heart

How do we get this "Jesus heart?" As it was for King Saul, this new heart is a gift from God. Like Saul, He gives it to us because we have an anointing, a work to do for Him. Unlike Saul, we must learn how to nurture this heart so that it does not grow cold and useless. Knowing that the contents of the heart will eventually be revealed in speech and behavior allows us to understand each other better.

- Pain in the heart makes a person bitter.
- Shame in the heart makes a person critical.
- Sadness in the heart makes a person depressed.
- Discouragement in the heart makes a person pessimistic.

- Anger and bitterness in the heart makes a person mean.
- Unbelief in the heart brings spiritual defeat.

On and on we can go. Knowing these things informs our prayers for that person and helps us deal with them in grace. The good news is the opposite is also true:

- A healed heart can pour out healing speech.
- A restored heart can help a person be appreciative of others.
- Joy in the heart makes someone the kind of person who lifts the spirits of others.
- Faith in the heart helps us be faith-building and optimistic and encouraging.
- Peace in the heart makes a person into a peacemaker.
- Jesus in the heart fills a person's mouth with praise!

Commanding Your Thinking

Surely Paul knew the teaching of Jesus about the abundance of the heart as the source of what we say and do. His words to the Philippians:

Philippians 4:8-9
Finally, brethren, whatsoever things are true,
whatsoever things are honest, whatsoever things are just,
whatsoever things are pure, whatsoever things are lovely,
whatsoever things are of good report; if there be any virtue, and if
there be any praise, think on these things. Those things, which ye
have both learned, and received, and heard, and seen in me, do:
and the God of peace shall be with you.

What is Paul saying to worship team members? He is saying this: "Learn to command your thinking." Control what you feed your heart! The world is full of messages that seek residence in our hearts; we have to be smart about what we invite into our most private thoughts. We must say with the Psalmist:

Psalm 101:3
I will set no wicked thing before mine eyes...

This means all manner of video, film, television, text, or visual art; if it is wicked, we don't need to watch it. God made us so that we remember what we have seen; educators call this the eye-gate and it works. At some level we mentally record what we have looked upon and to see it in the dark on a big screen with powerful music playing makes it go deep into our hearts These things will resurface to the conscious mind at the worst of times both waking and sleeping.

On the positive side, we can make this educational process work for us, helping us fill our hearts with good things. These things need to make up the abundance of our hearts:

- True things,
- Honest things,
- Pure things,
- Beautiful things,
- Beneficial things,
- Virtuous things, and
- The praises of God.

These wonderful things will fill our hearts and expand our passion for God and our compassion for people. We are commanded to think on these things. That means this must be an intentional practice. We need to find good books, good music, and good films to put into the storehouse of the heart. We need to go places where we can read the book of Creation to fill our hearts with God's beauty and peace. These internal things will take root in our hearts and beautify the music we make together as a worship team.

CONCLUSION

The members of the worship team live in the dynamic center between their inner selves and their public selves. The whole point is to worship the Lord in front of the church inviting them to join us. To do this well, the heart of each team member must constantly be loaded with good things. We must fill our hearts with Jesus so that His praise can be heard by those who hear us.

DISCUSSION QUESTIONS

1. Discuss the statement that worship is expressed in various forms of art.

2. What are some of the things artists learn from culture that they have to unlearn for worship arts?

3. Discuss the relationship between the internals and externals of worship leadership.

4. What are the two meanings given to "a man after God's own heart?"

5. How does the heart of King David compare to the Heart of Jesus?

6. What are the positives and negatives of the statement, "From the abundance of the heart the mouth speaks?

7. What is involved in "commanding your thinking?"

Worship from a Heart full of Praise Is More than Music!

Chapter Nine

Ephesians 2:19-22
Now therefore ye are no more strangers and foreigners,
but fellow citizens with the saints, and of the household of
God; And are built upon the foundation of the apostles and
prophets, Jesus Christ himself being the chief corner stone; in
whom all the building fitly framed together groweth unto an
holy temple in the Lord: In whom ye also are builded together
for an habitation of God through the Spirit.

INTRODUCTION
A PARTNERSHIP FOR MINISTRY

The Tabernacle Moses and the People of God built in the
wilderness can be seen as a metaphor for effective ministry.
Consider these elements:

- Moses had the plan of God, given to Him on the heights
  of Mt. Sinai.

- The People had the skills of a great civilization, gained
  in Egypt. They went into Egypt as a nation of herdsmen.
  Generations later, they emerged from Egypt as a nation
  of craftsmen.

- Moses and the People had the riches of Egypt as materials
  to build the Tabernacle.

Building Our Tabernacle

Each worship leader and worship team minister has to build a life to serve as the New Covenant realization of this Old Covenant structure—the Habitation of God in our Wilderness. Consider these elements:

- We have the Plans of God—the Word of God and the leadership of the Holy Spirit.

- We have talents from God that we have developed into skills that are useful to the Lord. These skills are often acquired in the world—the music education system, and technical training courses. We, too are a nation of craftsmen.

- As Christian artists, we plunder the riches of the world to master the musical styles and technical facilities designed to promote the wickedness of the age and use them instead to minister to the Lord in Praise and Worship and to tell the Jesus Story to the world.

To build this type of life, each worship team member must do this: answer the call to ministry!

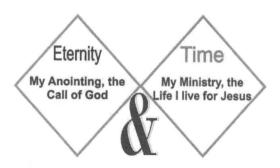

HEARING THE CALL OF GOD

The Central Fact of Your Life

You have an anointing from God! This calling is the central fact of your life. When you stand before the Lord and see your life's work tried by fire,[1] this will be an issue: What did you do with the call of God on your life? God designed you and built you with specific works in mind. Consider these verses:

Ephesians 2:10
For we are his workmanship, created in Christ Jesus unto good works, which God hath before ordained that we should walk in them.

1 John 2:27
But the anointing which ye have received of him abideth in you, and ye need not that any man teach you: but as the same anointing teacheth you of all things, and is truth, and is no lie, and even as it hath taught you, ye shall abide in him.

Psalm 16:11
Thou wilt shew me the path of life: in thy presence is fullness of joy; at thy right hand there are pleasures for evermore.

Finding and following your anointing is the Path of Life referred to in Psalm 16. How do these verses affect worship team members?

- **Ephesians 2:10:** You are God's creation, created to do certain things. You do not earn your salvation through these works but you serve the Lord and mankind through them. The Lord has a plan for you to walk. In His will, you will walk from task to task. Others who are walking their own paths will come alongside you and together you will walk and work. Others will cross your path for a single project and then each of you will continue on your way.

---

1 Corinthians 13-15

- **1 John 2:27:** In the things God has called you to do for
Him, you will have an inner source of knowledge and
wisdom. There will be aspects of the ministry that you
will simply know without ever needing a teacher. How
is this possible? Because the Holy Spirit is your teacher.
This inner ability to grow in understanding happens
through diligent study and it happens in the challenging
moments of ministry. Of course, this is not to say that
you don't need teachers; God has made it clear that we
all need teachers and we should all be teachers. In the
area of your calling, you will learn things directly from
the Lord in addition to what you learn from teachers.
These things should be tested by the Word. The Holy
Spirit will not contradict Himself.

- **Psalm 16:11:** The call of God on your life is the blessed,
abundant life you were put on this earth to live. Obeying
the call of God brings the fullness of joy as we walk this
earth. When this life is done, we can enter into the joys of
the Lord where there are pleasures forevermore.

Until then, there is much to do for the Lord Jesus! We must
never stop learning our craft and the principles of spirituality.
Every day is a growth day. Every night is a time of reflection
back on the day spent in the will of God, doing what He has
called us to do, and walking the Path of Life

How do we discover our Anointing?

Jesus tells us to take up our cross, deny ourselves, and
follow Him. The cross represents the will of God for our lives.
For Jesus, it meant Calvary, the Empty Tomb, and Ascension to
the Throne of Heaven. For us, our cross is the will of God for
us. The first clues are our natural interests. Since childhood, we
have been attracted to certain pursuits. At first, it was play, then
it became education until the time when we had to choose how
we would make a living. Many people make a living at what
interests them. Others have jobs that are of little interest to them
so they take up hobbies that interest them. Sometimes the call

of God is our vocation and sometimes it is just a commanding interest in our lives. Many musicians make music as a hobby while making a living at something else. The good news is, your anointing can be in the area of your hobby. Many worship team members serve the Lord as an avocation and not for a living.

Look for grace in your life. God will lead you to prepare the skills needed to fulfill your calling. Looking back, you can see patterns of grace that God sent you to lead you to the life you now lead:

- The piano or guitar lessons you took as a child,
- The musical home or family that nurtured you,
- The middle school and high school bands, choirs, and orchestras when you were a student,
- The music you were drawn to and wanted to learn to sing or play,
- The tech operators who let you watch over their shoulders,
- The school and church productions where you discovered your talents, and many other examples of God's grace.

God has always known why He put you on this earth and He has been actively leading you all the way. All of these graces came your way without you making them happen.

Now, as an adult, you must take the initiative to continue developing your skills. Some singers and players seem to think that whatever they learned before adulthood is the extent of their knowledge for life. It isn't true! You have not been given a life sentence! Keep learning. Keep practicing. Keep up! God has more for you to learn and more for you to do.

Seeking God's Call

If you are still unsure of the call of God on your life there is something else you can do, something that is a sure-fire solution: seek the call of God! Ask God to show you what He has put you on this earth to do. God's will is not a secret. He wants you to know His will and to be busy and happy doing His will. Here are the indicators:

- What does God bless in all your efforts for Him?
- In what endeavors does God seem to leave you to your own devices?
- Do your leaders affirm you in certain activities? Good leaders are always looking for the flow of the power of God in someone's life.
- What gives you joy and peace and a sense of satisfaction?
- What frustrates you when you fall short of your goals over and over?

These considerations point out what God has called you to do and what may be just your own ambition. Ambitions outside of our anointing can spring from problems deep in our wounded souls. The call of God is motivated by a desire to serve the Lord Jesus. Our ambitions can spring from desires to prove our worth or disprove someone's opinion of us or any number of compulsions that Jesus wants to heal before He can use us in the ministry.

Worship is the key to finding God's will

The prophet Isaiah is perhaps the most eloquent writer in the Old Testament. He was not born to this position. He was simply a historian, writing the deeds of his hero, King Uzziah. His hero did have a remarkable life. He became king as a child and ruled for many years. He made improvements of all kinds to the safety and productivity of Israel. In the later years of his reign, he began to envy the relationship the priests had with God. He was not satisfied with his anointing as king and sought to usurp the ministry of the priests. God's judgment on him was complete and he lost everything. Meanwhile, his young biographer had no good ending for his story. At this point in a life-changing moment of worship, Isaiah received his true calling. Like the disciples centuries later who changed the world because they had seen the Risen Jesus, Isaiah was granted a vision of heaven. He saw the Lord, high and lifted up! His life was changed in a two-step process:

1. He saw his unworthiness in the light of God's glory.

2. He heard God calling him to a specific work.

For us, as well, the will of God is revealed in the throne room of God. We need to attend to worship for to do so is to enter the Throne Room of Heaven. At first, our unworthiness will overwhelm us, but in the midst of heaven's music, we will eventually hear the voice of the Father *seeking us!* Listen to Isaiah's testimony, "Also I heard the voice of the Lord, saying, whom shall I send, and who will go for us?" Seeing His glory, hearing His call, there was only one proper answer "Here am I; send me." This story is worth reading:

Isaiah 6:1-9

In the year that king Uzziah died I saw also the Lord sitting upon a throne, high and lifted up, and his train filled the temple. Above it stood the seraphims: each one had six wings; with twain he covered his face, and with twain he covered his feet, and with twain he did fly. And one cried unto another, and said, Holy, holy, holy, is the Lord of hosts: the whole earth is full of his glory. And the posts of the door moved at the voice of him that cried, and the house was filled with smoke. Then said I, Woe is me! for I am undone; because I am a man of unclean lips, and I dwell in the midst of a people of unclean lips: for mine eyes have seen the King, the Lord of hosts. Then flew one of the seraphims unto me, having a live coal in his hand, which he had taken with the tongs from off the altar: And he laid it upon my mouth, and said, Lo, this hath touched thy lips; and thine iniquity is taken away, and thy sin purged. Also I heard the voice of the Lord, saying, Whom shall I send, and who will go for us? Then said I, Here am I; send me. And he said, Go, and tell this people, Hear ye indeed, but understand not; and see ye indeed, but perceive not.

This is why worship is so important! Every service can be an "Isaiah 6" service for someone.

Really, finding God's will should be a constant emphasis in the public worship and small group life of the church. As was stated earlier, this is the central fact of our lives both here and in eternity. When we stand before Jesus, nothing else will matter.

Someone who sings or plays music and someone who loves the technical aspects of worship ministry can be operating in their anointing. But, how can we know for sure? The important factor is the flow of the power of God. Just to be skillful at the crafts is not enough; we must learn to release our skills to the plans, purposes, and power of the Holy Spirit.

FOLLOWING THE CALL OF GOD

Knowing the call of God on our lives sets up a course of action. This is the proper place for ambition. It is proper to have great ambition within the area of your anointing. There are skills to be gained, mastered, and maintained. There are concepts to discover, articulate, and develop. There are relationships to form, share, and maintain. There is a field of study to begin or continue.

There are training events to attend or tend to individually. There is practice and rehearsal; these are not the same thing:

- Practice is what we do on our own to prepare for rehearsal or performance.

- Rehearsal is what we do together to prepare for performance.

There are disciplines to which we must submit, both personal and group behaviors that increase productivity, save time, and ensure quality. There are dynamics of leadership and what we might call "followship." Each team member must submit to the leader and be a leader by example to other team members.

Mary of Bethany.[1]

One of the most important stories in the life of Jesus concerns itself with Mary of Bethany, sister of Martha and Lazarus. At a crucial moment when Jesus and His men were resting in their home, Mary produced an alabaster container of an expensive perfume. Alabaster is a soft, white stone used to make containers for precious things. This jar had more than a sentimental value; it had a street value. It was worth a year's wages for a common laborer. Mary broke it open and poured it on Jesus. None of the disciples were paying Mary any mind but the aroma of the ointment filled the room. Led by Judas, the disciples rebuked her and called her worship a waste. Jesus rebuked them and declared that what she had done would forever be linked to the preaching of the Gospel. His direct words of commendation to Mary are significant in our study of the anointing.

- Leave her alone!
- She has done what she could.
- She has done a beautiful thing to Me.

What can worship team members learn from this incident?

- Jesus loves our full-hearted worship!
- He only holds us responsible for what we can do.
- Jesus appreciates the beauty we create as we worship Him.
- Our worship should have "a street value." Our music should be well done, well chosen, and worthy of the Lord.
- Our worship should be the best we have to give.
- We should hold nothing back in our adoration of and obedience to God.

This story should remain in the mind of every worship team member as a constant challenge to authentic worship before the Lord.

---

1   Matthew 26; Mark 14; John 12

One more thing to remember about the anointing—it grows. As we obey the Lord, He notices. It has been well said that "ministry leads to ministry." Do not be afraid to take the lesser role; you never know where it may lead. Take joy in the ministry of others. This type of humility will lead you to where the Lord wants you to be. Remember that humility is the essence of worship and pride is the antithesis of worship.

LIVING IN THIS PARTNERSHIP

Even without the ministry of the Holy Spirit, making music bonds the group together in powerful ways. When we add the anointing of the Holy Spirit, the bonding is even deeper and stronger. Just as there is a partnership between skill and anointing, the worship team is also a partnership. Just as in a musical ensemble there are many instruments and voice parts that must fit together into a single performance, in the church, there are many functioning parts to the ministry machine. Your gifts and abilities fit together with those of the other team members to build something bigger than any of you could ever create on your own.

This doesn't happen by accident. It happens when we are intentional about worship team ministry. Here are a few guidelines for being a good team member:

- Never envy the anointing or ministry of another team member. This is poison. Enjoy your own anointing and tend to it. This will keep you busy and out of trouble. Rejoice in the prominence of others.
- Never stop learning your craft—be a climber, not a camper. As Paul said, "I press on…"[1]
- Sometimes you should operate at the outer limits of your skills. Comfort zones are deadly. We do not grow when we remain within the safety zone of our present skills. To live by faith means to live in the place where if God doesn't do the work, it won't get done. You will surprise

1   Philippians 3:12 NKJV

yourself if you challenge yourself in this way—and you won't get bored.

- Do not impose your personal artistic needs on the ministry of the team. The team does not exist to serve you musically; it exists as your opportunity to serve God. If there is not enough music in worship team ministry to satisfy the musician in you, find some community outlet that will. Community bands, choirs, theatre groups need Christians in their ranks. You can keep growing musically and be a witness at the same time.

- Guard your devotional life—stay deep in the Jesus Story. It is the source of everything.

- Expect to hear directly from the Holy Spirit in the issues of life. The Bible is your primary source. Don't let too many people and their opinions get between you and Jesus. When you know your Bible well, you can tell the difference between the voice of the Spirit within and any other voices. As a Holy-Royal Priest you can tell the difference between the holy and the profane.[1]

- Keep an eye out for the next generation. Somebody helped you along when you were young. Do your part to keep this thing going.

- Be an encourager of your other team members. The day will come when you will need their encouragement.

- Never participate in team gossip or entertain critics of the leadership of the church. If issues arise, remember what the Bible teaches.[2] We are commanded not to gossip and we are commanded to pray for our leaders.

CONCLUSION

The call of God on our lives is an eternal concern. It is the key to a happy, productive life on earth and to our rewards in heaven. The Lord has made repeated invitations:

1   Ezekiel 22:26
2   Hebrews 13:17

- James 1:5: "If you lack wisdom, ask of God…"
- Isaiah 55:6: "Seek the Lord while He wills to be found…"
- Isaiah 30:21: "You will hear a voice…this is the way, walk ye in it…"
- John 15:16: "You have not chosen me, but I have chosen you and ordained you…"
- John 10:27: "My sheep hear my voice…"

His will for you is not a secret. He is seated on His throne with the order written out. He is waiting on you to get close enough to Him to hear His voice. A highly effective worship team is filled with people who are following the call of God on their lives.

DISCUSSION QUESTIONS

1. Discuss the metaphor of the Tabernacle as a model for the life of ministry.
2. What is meant by the statement: "Your calling is the central fact of your life?"
3. Discuss ways to discover your anointing.
4. Elaborate on the role of worship in hearing the call of God.
5. Discuss the difference between ambition and anointing.
6. What do we learn from Mary of Bethany?
7. Discuss the guidelines for being a good team member.

We are called to Worship God and It Is More than Music!

Chapter Ten

THE DYNAMIC CENTER

> **John 4:23-24**
> But the hour cometh, and now is, when the true worshipers shall worship the Father in spirit and in truth: for the Father seeketh such to worship him. God is a Spirit: and they that worship him must worship him in spirit and in truth.

INTRODUCTION
LIVING IN THE BOTH/AND WORLD OF WORSHIP LEADERSHIP

We live at the moment in history when Western Civilization is shaking off one worldview and embracing another. Modernists say this is an Either/Or world. Post-Modernists say it is a Both/And world. The church is shaking off a rational faith that tended to marginalize the supernatural and embracing a dynamic spirituality that welcomes a faith full of paradox and mystery and signs and wonders, both the spiritual and the rational.

- Modernists say that truth is linear (A+B=C) and facts are on those things which are visible, measurable, provable, repeatable, rational.

- Post-modernists say that truth is dynamic (A+B=Orange) and facts are relative, random, situational, and above all, personal.

Each of these approaches to life is replete with error and while the way may seem right, it leads only to destruction.[1] What is the true way? It is the way of Spirit and Truth—the Jesus Way. "Spirit and Truth" is more than just a worship philosophy; it is the way to live for God in this world! Our lives must be both rational and spiritual. When rationality is inadequate, we have spirituality. Our Spirituality, while not totally dependent upon reason, is reasonable when mixed with faith in the Word of God. It is not Either/Or; it is Both/And.

In this chapter, we will go into greater detail with the fundamental concept of this book—the truth about polarities: opposite propositions that are not in conflict with each other but are both true. We live in the dynamic center of powerful, complimentary truths.

UNDERSTANDING POLARITIES

The Planetary View

The planet earth is polarized. The North Pole pulls from the top of the world making the water in the Northern Hemisphere swirl clockwise. The South Pole pulls from down under and makes water in the Southern Hemisphere spin counterclockwise when it drains. In the middle, there is a line called the Equator. This is the dynamic center of the earth. The line is not fixed because it moves according to the forces acting upon it. At the Equator, water drains straight down. Hurricanes spin clockwise north of the Equator and counterclockwise to the south. The forces of each pole are so strong storms cannot cross the dynamic center.

1   Proverbs 16:25

The Polarities of Worship: Eternal and Temporary

In the same way as the earth whirls on its axis, worship spins between two strong poles: the eternal and the temporary. As stated earlier, worship is rooted in the eternal while it unfolds in time.

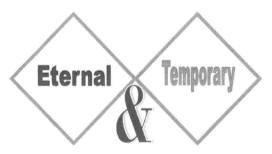

Worship moves between the pull of the eternal and the push of the cultural or temporary. As earthbound, time-bound human beings, we seek to enter the Throne Room of Heaven by joining the Heavenly hosts in worship: "Holy, Holy, Holy!"[1] We do this with our music, our language, and with our hearts—all temporary things. These are the only tools we have for this work. They can be sanctified by prayer and the anointing of the Spirit, just as the Tabernacles and Temples were in the Old Testament. In the New Covenant, we are the Temple of the Spirit[2], so we present our bodies to God as Living Sacrifices.[3] The Lord is faithful to His promise to be enthroned upon our praise and we are there—standing time-bound in eternity, worshiping at the dynamic center![4]

As human beings and not angels, the temporary elements of our culture are much more familiar to us than the eternal things in heaven. Without effort on our part, we tend to give the temporary things the lead in our thinking. After all, this is our music, our language, our culture. It flows from a place deep in our hearts. Our job is to judge the temporary by the eternal. Our preferences must be challenged by those of the God we want to worship.

1   Hebrews 12:22-24
2   1 Corinthians 3:16
3   Romans 12:1-2
4   Psalm 22:3

> **1 Thessalonians 5:16-23**
> Rejoice evermore. Pray without ceasing.
> In every thing give thanks: for this is the will of God in Christ
> Jesus concerning you. Quench not the Spirit. Despise not
> prophesyings. Prove all things; hold fast that which is good.
> Abstain from all appearance of evil. And the very God of
> peace sanctify you wholly; and I pray God your whole spirit
> and soul and body be preserved blameless unto the coming of
> our Lord Jesus Christ.

There will be more about this when we get to chapter 12.

WORSHIP LEADING POLARITIES

Skill and Anointing

This polarity has already been thoroughly discussed but it is important to remind team members of its importance and its place in this exposition of worship leading polarities. We do not lead with skill alone but with the power of the Holy Spirit. Neither do we relinquish our artistry as if it were unimportant. Our skill shapes the flow of the Spirit within us.

Artistry and Ministry

Closely related to the polarity of skill and anointing is the polarity of Artistry and Ministry. This is a polarity of motivation.

When we make music it is both an artistic endeavor and an attempt to perform a ministry. Music making and the technical support of musical teams is demanding work. It involves years of training and experience in the past as well as intense concentration in the moment. Such high skill levels of performance spring from strong motivations. For artists, the art matters. For technicians, the tech matters. Excellence in these areas is expected, creating pressure to perform on cue.

In the music world or in the concert or video world, excellence is the primary goal. In the ministry, excellence is a means to an end, not an end in itself. We produce excellent art with effective technical support toward a higher purpose—the worship of God and/or the telling of the Jesus Story. This means our art is what is called "functional art." Its success or failure is judged by more than artistic or technical standards alone. We must judge how well the presentation serves its goal. In this way worship leading is both art and ministry.

Praise and Worship

As we discussed previously, these terms are not synonyms; they are complementary but different in essence and in purpose. In a worship service, the team will be called upon to lead in praise and to lead in worship. The Praise-to-Worship sequence becomes an important reference point for the artists and technicians on the team. When the team is leading the congregation in praise, the tech must support this function.

When the ministry changes to worship, so must the tech. This is also true for the worship planners. If we follow the Tabernacle/temple model, each worship set should be a journey from Praise to Worship. Likewise, when the function of the music is prayer, supporting the whole congregation at the altars or for a service of Holy Communion, the prayer function of the music and tech should be maintained. When the service moves to celebration, the music and tech must follow.

Preparation and Presentation

The Polarity of Preparation and Presentation deals with the attitudes of individual team members. Some people value presentation over preparation. To these team members, rehearsals are not as important as services. They may miss rehearsals, or be late for them, or see their role as one of preparing their own part. Others see rehearsals as just as important as services. These are the most valuable team members. They practice to prepare for rehearsals. They do not miss times of preparation and are generally there on time. They understand that this is more than simply learning "their part." They have a leadership role to the other members of the team. These are the team members the leaders and the church can really count on. The choice is not between preparing or not preparing; it is the powerful synthesis of both preparation and presentation that does the work of the ministry week after week, season after season.

Planning and Spontaneity

Different congregations and traditions have differing attitudes toward the polarity of Planning and Spontaneity. Some groups prepare every minute of every service well in advance while others prepare only a basic outline of the service and improvise all the connecting events. We are not faced with a choice of these two things. Our ongoing challenge is to find the dynamic center between the two. The truth is this: the better prepared the team is, the more spontaneous the worship team can be in the service. When we have carefully prepared a service, it is not a failure in planning when God surprises us in a service—it is a delightful gift. Planning worship is an exercise in prophecy; we foresee a service and plan what we will do in that service. For those whose services lean toward spontaneity, it is good to plan what I call flex points in the service, where everyone can follow the leadership of the Spirit in unplanned ways. How wonderful it would be if the Lord would break into our routine with a visitation from above! Both the music team and the tech team have the greatest challenges when this happens.

Tradition and Innovation

Perhaps the greatest potential for conflict over worship is addressed by this polarity. Tradition is a powerful force in the church and rightfully so. There is an inertia in public worship; people want what is familiar to them. As Tevye says in *Fiddler on the Roof*, "Because of our traditions, every one of us knows who he is and what God expects him to do." This tension is most readily seen in the selection of the music for worship. People who value tradition more than innovation prefer the songs they already know. People who prefer innovation over tradition will want all the new songs and song forms they can get. Again, the scripture calls for both the old and the new.

- The Psalms, the Prophet Isaiah, and John on the Patmos either call for new songs or report that even in heaven they are singing new songs.

- The Psalms call for an inter-generational conversation on the glory of the Lord.

Psalm 145:4
One generation shall praise thy works to another, and shall declare thy mighty acts.

The primary method of past generations to speak after they have left the scene is through the art they have left behind. The current generation speaks through today's songwriters and past generations speak through the songs of songwriters of their generation. It takes both kinds of songs to hear everything the Spirit is saying to the church.

Revelation 2:7
He that hath an ear, let him hear what the Spirit saith unto the churches.

We need to hear everything the Spirit is saying to us so we need both tradition and innovation. Also, a service of worship has three necessary time frames:

1. Past: Remembering God's works in history: the Gate of Thanksgiving,

2. Present: Encountering Jesus today: His promise to be with us; Praise, prayer, giving,

3. Future: Preparing for the future: Preaching of the Word; congregational prayer.

Both traditional songs and new songs can fulfill these time-sensitive parts of the service. So, this too is a Both/And polarity.

Transcendence and Immanence

In public worship, the church needs to encounter both the "otherness" of God and the "nearness" of God. In theologian-speak, this is called God's Transcendence and His Immanence.

- He is God Almighty, the Lord of Hosts and
- He is God with Us, the Friend who is closer than a brother.

It is not uncommon for a single service to express both of the aspects of God's presence.

- In the Thanksgiving/Praise portion of the service, we proclaim His Majesty.

In the Adoration/Communion/Worship part of the service, we experience the tenderness of His nearness.

The danger comes when through personal preference either the greatness of God or the tenderness of God is routinely emphasized at the omission of the complimentary revelation. The fact is God is both on a throne of majesty and He is closer to us than our very breath. As we are led by the Spirit of God, we lead both kinds of worship. There are services where the Spirit will lead us to major in the celebration of only one of these characteristics. This is good and we must always follow the leadership of the Spirit. The overall worship liturgy expressed over time should celebrate both God's transcendence and His Immanence.

Private Worship and Public Worship

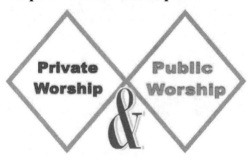

The next chapter will deal with private worship in detail. Here we must include this polarity in this list. Some worship leaders have said that we cannot lead people somewhere we haven't been and it is true. Worship team members should prepare for the intense ministry of the weekend by spending time with God every day. In the Sermon on the Mount, Jesus called it the Closet of Prayer, or in modern translations, the Secret Place. For this, we need a method and that will be part of Chapter 11. The point here is this: We must not choose public worship over private worship; we must have both.

Exposition and Celebration

Public worship is more than congregational music; there is also a role for the public reading of Scripture.[1] This will always

1   1 Timothy 4:13

involve the tech team for the projection of the verses and may involve the singers as public readers. This part of worship can be called "Exposition," the presentation of information. Preaching would also fall under this category as would announcements.

From the world of art music, we can learn the power of the use of the spoken word in conjunction with the word that is sung. In opera two types of vocal music are used:

1. Recitative—songs that are practically spoken; they advance the plot and give the audience necessary information.

2. Aria—a song designed for a major character to sing in celebration of the information given in the recitative.

A worship service is like this. There are times when information is being delivered to the people and there are other times when the people celebrate what has been said. Traditional strophic hymns, those with stanzas and a refrain, actually function as both exposition and celebration; the stanzas give information and the refrain celebrates it. Exposition and Celebration are really opposites and demand totally different art and technical support but the church needs both.

CONCLUSION

A certain term has been avoided in this chapter—balance. Often, when discussing polarities, the concept of balancing the two opposites will be mentioned. However, with the issue of worship, balance is not a worthy goal. It speaks of score-keeping and people pleasing; these are artificial measurements. There are times when the Spirit will lead us to be out of balance. He wants us to major in one pole of the polarity in a particular service. This can be readily seen in consideration of the Transcendence / Immanence polarity. It is altogether proper for the Lord to lead us in a complete service celebrating His nearness. Perhaps in the time of a natural emergency or a congregational loss, this unbalanced service would still be correct. At another time, the

Spirit may wish to impress on us the majesty of God and de-emphasize His Immanence. This, too, would still be proper. The point is not to be balanced but to be sensitive to the leadership of the Holy Spirit.

Along the way, the worship team should be aware of these polarities and guard their hearts from inappropriate emphasis or neglect. Remember, the point is to find the Dynamic Center for each service! When we do this, we will keep Jesus at the center of our worship.

DISCUSSION QUESTIONS

1. Discuss the differences between Either/Or and Both/And reasoning.
2. What is meant by polarities and how does the earth illustrate this?
3. Discuss the Artistry/Ministry polarity.
4. How do preparation and presentation relate to each other?
5. What is the relationship between planning and spontaneity?
6. What is one way to express the dynamic center between Tradition and Innovation?
7. Explain the Transcendence/Immanence polarity.

At the Dynamic Center, Worship Is More than Music!

Chapter Eleven

IN the SECRET PLACE

> **Matthew 6:6**
> But thou, when thou prayest, enter into thy closet, and when thou hast shut thy door, pray to thy Father which is in secret; and thy Father which seeth in secret shall reward thee openly.

INTRODUCTION
IN THE PUBLIC PLACE

Leading a congregation in worship is of necessity a public ministry. It is inevitable that as we present the music and technology of worship, we are also presenting ourselves. When everything goes well, there is a sense of public accomplishment. This is not a bad thing at all; we should take joy in doing our ministry well. We must also keep our hearts centered on the Lord and not let public appreciation become a goal. Our principal objective is to please the Lord the way Mary of Bethany did, winning the splendid commendations of Jesus: "She has done a beautiful thing to Me," and "She has done what she could." Pleasing the Lord is the true goal of the worship team.

There is a private power source for this public success. In the Sermon on the Mount, Jesus called this the Closet of Prayer.[1] Modern translations call it "The Secret Place." Jesus said the Father was there, in the Secret Place. We go there in private worship.

---

1 Matthew 6:6

- There is no congregation of people (although myriads of angels may attend.)

- The Father is the only audience.

- The lighting is room lighting perhaps enhanced by candles or the setting or rising sun.

- The liturgy of our worship is the Word of God and the contents of our heart.

In this place of holy solitude, we are prepared for ministry in the Public Place. Jesus said the Father will reward in public what is done in secret. If worship team members intend to be effective on the church platform, they had better learn how to be effective here in the Secret Place.

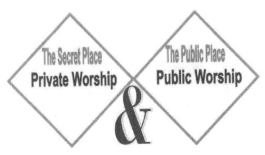

We Need the Secret Place

In the twenty-first century, the need for private prayer is evident in the church of the Lord Jesus Christ. We have an abundance of forms, but sometimes we lack power.[1] Where can we go to find the power? Who can we turn to for an example of how to live the powerful Christian life that changes our world?

- The apostles, the first followers of the Lord Jesus, changed their world. In less than three hundred years the first church grew from 120 leaders in the upper room to a universal army that was the first to conquer the Roman Empire.

---

1   II Timothy 3:5

- In the Protestant Reformation, leaders returned to the Scriptures for guidance on how to be the People of God and their world was changed.

- In the 19th Century, leaders sought out scriptural truth in the face of Darwinian evolution, Freudian psychology, and higher criticism of the Bible to bring about a world-changing revival of biblical Christianity known as Evangelicalism.

- One hundred years ago the Pentecostals came on the scene with their Apostolic Reformation and the world is still being changed today.

What do they have in common?—private prayer, prayer in the Secret Place.

The Father is there, Jesus said. He will reward openly what we do secretly, privately with no possibility of the acclaim of men. The character of Christ is imparted to us in the Secret Place.

- Here the Refiner's Fire burns hottest and the Launderer's Soap cleanses deepest.[1]
- Here, worshipers are changed from glory to glory as they behold the Lord.
- Here the call of the Father can be heard clearest.
- Here the compassion of Christ is imparted best.
- Here the Word of God dwells in us the richest.
- Here the power of the anointing of the Holy Spirit is gained.
- Here the world gets changed.

We need to rediscover the Secret Place. There are secrets here, long forgotten, that were familiar to the Apostles. These secret things may be as foreign to us as the robes and sandals world of Paul, Peter, and Jesus is to us. In this chapter, we will learn about prayer in the Secret Place—the power source behind success in the Public Place.

---

1 Malachi 3:1-3

THE LIFE OF PRAYER

> ## 1 Thessalonians 5:16-18 NKJV
> Rejoice always, pray without ceasing, in everything give thanks; for this is the will of God in Christ Jesus for you.

We all need to pray. Some need to pray more, others need to pray more regularly, some need to pray better, and others need to make a new start at the whole enterprise.

The words of Jesus and Paul challenge us and stir our hearts. Jesus says, "The Father is in the Secret Place of Prayer." Paul adds, "Pray without ceasing."[1] But how? Where do we find the Secret Place? How do we even attempt to build a life around prayer? These words have challenged believers since Jesus spoke them and Paul wrote them.

How is it possible to pray without ceasing? One answer is to frame the day in prayer with both morning and evening times of prayer. Another is to keep an internal dialogue in progress in your heart, listening for the voice of God in the world around you and giving Him praise and thanks for His love and care throughout the day. Work is also a form of prayer when we do our work as Paul tells us to in Colossians, with all our might, in the name of the Lord and unto God and not unto people. Constant prayer sanctifies life.

> ## Colossians 3:17; 23
> And whatsoever ye do in word or deed,
> do all in the name of the Lord Jesus, giving thanks to God
> and the Father by him. ...And whatsoever ye do, do it heartily,
> as to the Lord, and not unto men...

A Biblical Overview of the New Testament on Prayer

- Jesus' teaching on prayer in the Secret Place is the heart of the Sermon on the Mount and the Sermon on the Mount serves as a sort of constitution for the Kingdom of

---

1   I Thessalonians 5:17

God. Jesus spoke of a spiritual life that is only possible in the power of the Holy Spirit. Private prayer in The Secret Place is the furnace that forges such lives of steel. This is not the power-mongering prayer of the religious leaders of that day or the marketplace praying of the hypocrites or the theatrical giving of alms. This is Secret Place prayer, where no one hears or sees but the Father in Heaven.

- Paul has the authority to instruct us in the Life of Prayer. He was a man of continual prayer. He was schooled in Jewish prayer. When he became a Christian, he found a new, more intense and effective form of prayer when he learned to pray in the Holy Spirit. We see in the book of Acts the crisis moments of his life. We see him praying in jail at midnight, aboard ship in a storm, and in public ministry with great power and effect. In his letters to the churches, we get a glimpse of his private prayer life: with understanding and with the spirit, without ceasing, with great revelation, and with an expectation of signs and wonders. His powerful public life sprang from a powerful private life of prayer.

- Jesus brought a new era of relationship with God. He brought an understandable revelation of God the Father, a real forgiveness of sin through the cross and a real helper in the Holy Spirit. He said that worship, which includes prayer, would not be in ceremony and tradition alone. These can be performed outwardly with no sincere action of the heart. New Covenant worship, on the other hand, would be done in spirit and in truth.

This spirituality is internal before it is external. This is an inner spirituality of integrity, honesty, and humility formed by the Word of God, the truth that sets us free and is empowered by the Holy Spirit. This cannot be faked for God Himself is the object and He cannot be fooled. We need to learn from the Apostles!

THE FIRST CENTURY PRAYER PARADIGM

These people knew how to pray! The record in the Book of Acts is impressive. Prison doors yielded to the force of the prayers of the church. Buildings shook. Lame men walked. The gospel was preached in power. The church enjoyed unity and grew as the Lord gave the increase. The centuries following the time of the Apostles saw the sustaining power of the Holy Spirit in the lives of believers who served the Lord at the risk of their lives. Soon the Roman Empire itself fell before the prayers of the church. Jesus' words proved true: the gates of hell could not prevail before the people of God.

Yes, they prayed and served the Lord in their generation, but *how* did these first-century believers pray? Can we learn from them in the school of prayer? The Apostles and those who followed them had wonderful methods of prayer. Their prayer lives were rich and varied. I call their methods the Apostolic Prayer Paradigm.

Jesus and His followers were products of the Old Covenant prayer paradigm. This method featured two powerful modes of praying:

1. extemporaneous or simple prayer, conversing with God

2. fixed prayers from Scripture.

With the coming of the Holy Spirit on the Day of Pentecost, a third mode of prayer came into the devotional lives of the followers of Jesus—prayer in the Spirit. With the addition of prayer in the Spirit, the Apostolic Prayer Paradigm was complete. The fullness of this prayer life is available today. What do these terms mean?

Prayer in the Holy Spirit

To pray in the Spirit is to pray from our spirit, the deepest part of our heart, in the power of the Holy Spirit. This type of prayer is filled with the Word of God and with Faith. It springs from a heart filled with the Spirit of God. It is unlimited by our minds or even our vocabulary. With Prayer in the Spirit, our spirit bears witness with God's Spirit that we are God's children.[1]

The benefits of this mode of prayer are well known to believers around the world. Among the benefits are:

- to speak mysteries,[2]
- to be built up by the process,[3]
- to pray beyond the limits of human understanding,[4]
- to pray in the Spirit and also with the mind[5]
- to offer perfect praise to the Lord [6]
- to bring things gained in the Secret Place to the public service[7] and
- to intercede with specific details when those details are unknown to the intercessor.[8]

Prayer in the Spirit is the hope of the world!

Extemporaneous Prayer

A walk with someone is characterized by a conversation with them. Many beloved songs of the past speak eloquently of walking and talking with the Lord. This is an effective description of conversational prayer, a running conversation through the day and through the night, and an unending awareness of the voice of God in our spirits. Continual prayer flows from our ready access to the ear of God through faith. This powerful privilege was a part of Old Covenant spirituality and has intensified for us under the New Covenant because of the abiding presence of the Holy Spirit.

1   Romans 8:13
2   1 Corinthians 14:2-5
3   1 Corinthians 14:14
4   1 Corinthians 14:14
5   1 Corinthians 14:15
6   1 Corinthians 14:17 NKJV
7   1 Corinthians 14:26
8   Romans 8:26-27

Fixed Prayers from Scripture and Tradition

While the first two modes of ancient prayer are familiar to Evangelicals, Pentecostals, and charismatics, the third mode is not so familiar. In the seventeenth century, the radical reformers, groups like the Puritans, sought to reform the Reformation by eliminating all things that looked to them like Roman Catholicism. Evangelicalism is a descendant of these revivalists. Those who formed the founders of Evangelicalism threw out recited prayers as inherently unspiritual, insincere, and "Roman."

In reality, the use of written prayers is much older than Roman Catholic traditions. Their use goes back to the time of King David and was the common practice of Jesus, the disciples, and believers of the first four centuries of the church. The use of these prayers included praying the Psalms. It is intriguing to think of Jesus reciting these scriptures as prayers. No wonder he was ready with the answer to the lawyer's question about the greatest command; he prayed it every morning! Before Jesus prayed the psalms from the cross, "My God, my God, why have you forsaken me?"[1] and, "Into your hands I commit my spirit."[2] He had recited them countless times since childhood. The daily use of fixed Scripture prayers and the great classical prayers of the church can be an excellent structure for daily private worship.

With these three modes of prayer, the Apostolic Prayer Paradigm was complete. The Apostles prayed in three modes,

1. in the Spirit,
2. extemporaneously and
3. with fixed prayers from Scripture and tradition.

---

1   Psalm 22:1
2   Psalm 31:5

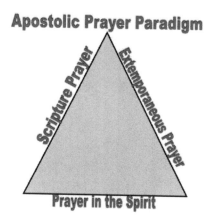

SECRETS OF THE SECRET PLACE

How do we learn to pray effectively in the Secret Place? It begins with an expansion of our definition of prayer. Prayer is more than just asking God for things; it is spending quality time with the Father, talking to Him and listening to Him. Next, we need to commit to a regular time of prayer. Finally, we need to expand our skill in prayer. We need to learn and practice these eight secrets.

1. Solitude: Get alone with God.

Being alone with God bars any possibility of performance praying. If another person can hear our words, this affects the way we pray. The first secret of the Secret Place is to be absolutely alone with the Father. Find a time, a chair, a room, a corner, or a couch in your home. This is your personal appointment with Abba Father. Most likely, your family will be happy to help you pray more!

2. Silence: Quiet your spirit before God.

Silence is the searchlight of the soul. The voice of the Lord is heard in the human spirit when we quiet our souls. Noise is the enemy of the Secret Place. I avoid music with word associations as background. If I am inwardly singing, I am not being silent. Our culture hates silence and our souls have been shaped in its image. But our spirit was created in the image of God and craves the silence of creation wherein is heard the voice of God. Together, these two secrets imply a schedule with quiet times of prayer set for each day.

3. Scripture: Recite the Word of God

Prayer is so much more than asking God for things. Praying the Scriptures has a vital role in the strengthening discipline. Today we need to reclaim this powerful discipline. In the ancient church, the leaders formed an axiom: "The Rule of Prayer is the Rule of Faith." In other words, what we pray reveals and forms what we believe. Great theology (right beliefs about God) springs from great doxology (proper praise of God). Today we also need to rehearse the revelation in Scripture of who God is and what He has promised. This is not "vain" repetition, but a purposeful rehearsal of truth so that it can go deep enough into us to set us free.

4. Spirit: Follow the leadership of the Holy Spirit.

Your practice of this type of praying varies with your personal experience of the Holy Spirit, but this is more than a denominational distinctive. The Holy Spirit helps believers pray—all of us. When we are alone with God and have quieted our souls and rehearsed the revelation of Scripture, the Holy Spirit is ready to lead us as we pray about whatever and whoever He brings to mind. It is good to keep a prayer list, but we should also listen for the voice of the Spirit calling us to pray for names and situations, not on our list.

5. Sincerity: Humility is essential.

True prayer and pride are mortal enemies. There is simply no way to fool God. If we speak a lie when we are praying we are not really praying and the Spirit tells us so. Prayer can be a process of peeling back layers of deception until we finally speak the truth. In the Secret Place, "God resists the proud and gives grace to the humble."[1] Humility is genuine; there are no

1   James 4:6; I Peter 5:5

mixed motives. According to James 1:5-8, mixed motives in prayer removes the possibility of answered prayer![1]

6. Speech: Pray out loud, not just inwardly.

While God certainly hears the silent cry of the heart, in the daily discipline of prayer we need to speak out loud. That's why we need to be alone with God. Each of us has things to say that only God should hear. Private prayer becomes therapeutic at this point. There is no reason to carry unexpressed pain in our hearts. Get it out! Let Abba Father deal with it! He knows all about it anyway. This is why the Psalms are important to us as prayers. Like the Psalmists, we may need to question God. We may need to complain or lament. While these prayers may not be appropriate for the community of faith, they are vital in the Secret Place! Our inner healing awaits the catharsis of prayer.

7. Song: A key to releasing faith is the prayer song.

When Jesus strode into the Temple, whip in hand and a stern rebuke on His lips, the issue was prayer in His Father's House. Not just any prayer, but songs of prayer. The word Isaiah used in the passage Jesus was quoting was *tepillah*,[2] the Hebrew word for hymn. To Jesus and the disciples, hymns were not old songs in hardbound books. They were songs or chants of prayer, usually the Scriptures themselves. Like our forebears who rode this country on horseback with their Bibles and their hymnals, we need to use great hymns and contemporary songs as prayers and we need to use the Psalms as prayers. In the plan of God melody and prayer are meant to flow together.

1   James 1:5-8 If any of you lack wisdom, let him ask of God, that giveth to all men liberally, and upbraideth not; and it shall be given him. But let him ask in faith, nothing wavering. For he that wavereth is like a wave of the sea driven with the wind and tossed. For let not that man think that he shall receive any thing of the Lord. A double minded man is unstable in all his ways.

2   tepillah OT:8605, (Strong's) (Vine's Expository Dictionary of Biblical Words, Copyright © 1985, Thomas Nelson Publishers.)

8. Supplicate: Ask, seek, knock.

Jesus teaches us to stay with it; to keep praying and never give up. We must be careful why we keep praying. It is not to impress God or to wear Him down. Jesus taught prayer as an exercise based on the sterling character of God. Heathens prayed with much repetition to appease a hostile God. Abba Father already knows what we need. Our prayers are repeated for a different reason. Prayer is spiritual warfare. While we cannot see the warfare at work in the spirit-realm when we are praying, it is happening. There is a record in the Old Testament of twenty-one days elapsing between the answer being sent and the answer being received—twenty-one days of angelic warfare.[1] We don't know why answers to prayer are sometimes delayed but we know what we should be doing: asking, seeking, and knocking with confidence in a God. 'If my words abide in you," Jesus said, "You shall ask what you will and it shall be done."[2] When we have God's will in a matter, we can confidently keep on asking, seeking and knocking in prayer.

THREE METHODS OF PRIVATE WORSHIP

All of this information is good, but how do we put it all together into a daily discipline? Here are three proven methods of Private Prayer:

Method Number One:
Bible Reading and Extemporaneous Prayer

- Systematic reading of Scripture in several places each day: Psalms/Proverbs; Old Testament; New Testament; Gospels/Acts
- Extemporaneous Prayer and a Prayer List.

Method Number Two
Daily Devotional and Extemporaneous Prayer

- Daily reading from a devotional book or an online devotional.
- PathofLifeDevotions.com (500+ word reading; selected scripture readings; prayer; song)

---

1 Daniel 10:12-13
2 John 5:7

- In 2018 I am writing "The Jesus Story" from each of the four Gospels.

Method Number Three
Prayer Book, Bible Reading, and Extemporaneous Prayer

- *The Book of Daily Prayer* presents a private service of worship for each day of the week and one for the evening. Based on the Book of Common Prayer, a staple of Protestant worship, this book collects ancient prayers from the Bible and from Christian Tradition.

- Time for systematic Bible reading is provided at a certain point in each service.

- Time for extemporaneous prayer for personal needs is also provided

CONCLUSION

There are four vital ministries of the Holy Spirit available to the believer as a result of effective private worship:

- The character of Christ is imparted to us in the secret place as the Refiner's Fire purifies and the Launderer's Soap cleanses.[1]

- In the secret place, the call of the Father can be heard.[2]

- Since secret place worship is an exercise in hope, the compassion of Christ is imparted to the worshiper in private worship. "Now hope does not disappoint, because the love of God has been poured out in our hearts by the Holy Spirit who was given to us."[3]

- In private worship, the Word of God dwells in us[4] and the power of the anointing of the Holy Spirit is acquired.[5]

1 Malachi. 3:1-3
2 Isaiah. 6:1-6
3 Romans. 5:5 NKJV
4 Colossians. 3:16
5 Ephesians. 1:15-21; 1 John 2:20, 27

In the secret place, the world is changed because it is here that we are changed. A highly effective worship team is faithful to the Secret Place of prayer.

DISCUSSION QUESTIONS

1. Discuss the relationship between private worship and public worship.

2. What are some of the blessings received in the Secret Place of Prayer?

3. How is it possible to pray without ceasing?

4. Discuss the teachings of Jesus on prayer.

5. What are the three modes of prayer in the Apostolic Prayer Paradigm?

6. How practical are the eight secrets of the Secret Place?

7. Discuss the three methods of Private Worship.

To be Alone with God Is More than Music!

Chapter Twelve

SEMPER REFORMANDA!

> **1 Thessalonians 5:21**
> Prove all things; hold fast that which is good.

INTRODUCTION
THE WORK THAT IS NEVER DONE

Each generation of worshipers has a particular work to do. They must take the traditions handed down to them and the innovations of their own generation and sift them by the Word of God. They must prayerfully and respectfully discard the temporary things that are passing away and reinforce the eternal things that must remain. Culture, the combination of personal preferences and group customs, is an essential element in public worship. In each generation, these cultural expressions effectively express the worship of the people who use them. Problems arise when the next generation, or the one after that, does not prefer the worship culture of their parents and grandparents. When the younger generations are not served well by the cultures they inherit, they invent their own. If their parents are not blessed by the new worship cultures of their offspring, the worship of God in spirit and truth is hindered by generational conflicts brought on by a clash of cultural preferences. In view of this, we must echo the question of Pastor James of the Jerusalem church and we must agree with the demand of the Apostle Paul and with his conclusion:

James 4:1

From whence come wars and fightings among you?

---

1 Corinthians 1:10; 3:3

Now I beseech you, brethren, by the name of our Lord Jesus
Christ, that ye all speak the same thing, and that there be no
divisions among you; but that ye be perfectly joined together
in the same mind and in the same judgment. ...For ye are yet
carnal: for whereas there is among you envying, and strife,
and divisions, are ye not carnal, and walk as men?

Neither James nor Paul soft-pedaled their view on conflicts
in the church; they are based in carnal values. Carnality leads to
strife and division. Spirituality leads to unity with diversity.

Are there solutions to this perpetual drama? We see this in
the stories of Abraham, Isaac, and Jacob:

- Abraham heard from God.
- He told Isaac about it, and
- Jacob had to wrestle with God for himself.

This is an oft-repeated historical pattern:

- A generation experiences a move of the Spirit and teaches
  both the Scriptural principles and their cultural practices
  to their children.

- The next generation improves on their parent's culture,
  perfecting and canonizing it—making it the accepted
  tradition.

- The next generation lives in a different world and does
  not appreciate the worship culture of their forebears and
  wishes to form its own worship culture.

- At this point, the older generation faces the choice of
  losing their children and grandchildren to the Kingdom
  or losing their own worship culture.

Neither of these outcomes is the perfect plan of God. What
is God's plan?

Unity with Diversity

The plan of God for worship mirrors everything God has created:

When we look at God's creation, we see an amazing variety of animals designed on a much smaller number of frames. The same is true for plant life and aquatic life. A cursory glance at the night sky reveals the same information—God loves variety! He loves diversity and He has created frameworks of unity upon which diversity can flourish.

- How many species of animals are built on the vertebrate design?

- How many kinds of birds fly on the same ingenious wing?

- How many creatures live in the water because God invented the gill?

One unifying idea results in countless individual creations: unity with diversity.

And so it should be with worship culture. It should be as diverse as the cultures within the congregation and as unified as the Scriptures themselves—Unity with Diversity. Instead of separating the generations into warring camps, worship culture should unite the generations into communities of shared truth and beauty. We must learn to celebrate each other's worship arts. This chapter will explore ways to see this counter-cultural miracle happen for your worship team and congregation.

Semper Reformanda!—Learning from the Protestant Reformers

These anointed men and women had to undo the work of more than 1000 years of worship ideas that were a mixture of the Word of God and the cultures of men. How did the church get to such a place of mixed motives and jumbled up ideas? The answers are many and complex but at the heart of them is this: people did not have access to the Bible. Illiteracy was the norm so the church took on the job of preserving the Scriptures (we have them to thank for this) and interpreting the scriptures—this was not so much of a blessing. Over the centuries, two unfortunate things happened:

1. Control of the Word of God became a political power source for an elevated priesthood, and,
2. The ideas of men were added to the Word of God and took on equal authority. The church canonized[1] culture. This also happened in the time of Christ:

Mark 7:6-7

He answered and said unto them, Well hath Esaias prophesied of you hypocrites, as it is written, This people honoureth me with their lips, but their heart is far from me. Howbeit in vain do they worship me, teaching for doctrines the commandments of men.

It was wrong for worshipers to canonize, that is, to give biblical authority, to their preferences as if they were Holy Scriptures. It was wrong then and it is wrong today. Let's learn from the leaders of the Protestant Reformation.

Protestant Reformers started translating the Bible into languages of the people and challenged the teachings of the church that were not biblical. This revolution, aided by the invention of the printing press, disrupted European civilization and divided the Western church into Catholic and Protestant.

---

1   To canonize an idea is to assign to it an authority equal to that of Scripture.

Eventually, four great principles of the Protestant Reformation emerged as the driving forces behind this spiritual renewal:

1. The Authority of Scripture, not the church,
2. Salvation by faith in Christ and not by works,
3. The Priesthood of all believers, not just an elevated few,
4. *Semper Reformanda!*—"Always Reforming."

The fourth great Reformation principle is not as well-known as the first three, but it is as important as the others. Without teaching a constant state of renewal by the Scriptures, the church is destined to flame up and flame out in an unending series of renewals and apostasies. Why? Because each renewal movement tends to think it is the last one. They got worship right so there is no need for further reformation.

We must be smarter than that. The truth is, the work of worship renewal is never completed by a single generation. It must be continued from generation to generation. Why? Not because the Bible changes, but because culture changes. This makes the knowledge of Bible truth more important than the knowledge of cultural trends. Let us find the Unity of the changeless Word of God and judge our worship cultures, old and new, by that standard. This spiritual unity will produce, as it always does in the hands of the Holy Spirit, a beautiful Diversity of expression and a Holy Counterculture of the young with the old in the peace of God.

STRATEGIES FOR CONSTANT REFORMATION

Before we get into these strategies, it is important to recognize the methodology of this constant worship reformation.

- We do not reform worship based on surveys of what people want in worship.
- We attempt to reform worship based on the study of what God wants us to do as it is revealed in the Bible.

- The role of the pastor in continuous worship renewal is to teach the Bible on worship. The Pastor must establish a context of continual renewal.
- The worship schedule of the church should not keep the generations apart but bring them together in significant ways.
- The church leadership must foster love between the old and the young as the Bible demands.

Titus 2:1-6

But speak thou the things which become sound doctrine: That the aged men be sober, grave, temperate, sound in faith, in charity, in patience. The aged women likewise, that they be in behaviour as becometh holiness, not false accusers, not given to much wine, teachers of good things; that they may teach the young women to be sober, to love their husbands, to love their children, to be discreet, chaste, keepers at home, good, obedient to their own husbands, that the word of God be not blasphemed. Young men likewise exhort to be sober minded.

With these spiritual guidelines, what are some strategies for continuous renewal?

Traditioning

2 Timothy 2:1-3

Thou therefore, my son, be strong in the grace that is in Christ Jesus. And the things that thou hast heard of me among many witnesses, the same commit thou to faithful men, who shall be able to teach others also. Thou therefore endure hardness, as a good soldier of Jesus Christ.

The dictionary does not recognize traditioning as a word but it is one used by theologians to describe how the values and beliefs of one generation are transmitted to the next. This is one of the most important functions of public worship. It is for this reason that beliefs are taught to believers with songs. Songs are marvelous little theology lessons with memorable tunes and words that rhyme. When we sing what we believe, it goes deep into our brain and, with the help of music and rhyme, it lodges there. This function may not be a conscious one or even be an intention of the worship leader and team, but it happens nonetheless.

As proof of this, stories abound of prisoners of war in solitary confinement who maintained their sanity through the songs and scriptures they had memorized. Victims of the terrible mental disorders that rob them of the memories of their lives will still remember the songs they sang in church. Research has shown there is a place in the brain where the music of our lives—that music that is most important to us—goes. Patients sometimes experience strokes where these memory banks are activated and this music plays for them. God made that place in the brain of every worshiper. It is our job to fill it with the best worship songs we can find!

The church must not leave traditioning to chance. This must be the intention of the teaching and discipleship ministries of the church. Foremost among these discipleship ministries is the public worship ministry. To simply program the most popular songs from the contemporary worship industry may or may not express the core beliefs of the church.

- Since worship songs are often songs of prayer, it is good to remember the ancient maxim, "The Rule of Prayer is the Rule of Faith."
- Just as praying great prayers builds great faith, singing great songs of truth writes those truths into the hearts of the people.

- Remember also the three-time frames of a worship service, past, present, and future. Singing great songs of faith can celebrate the past and prepare worshipers for the future while we are spending time with Jesus in the service.

An effective worship team ministers far beyond the power of music alone! This ministry is a connector between generations of faith.

From Generation to Generation

Psalm 79:13 ESV
But we your people, the sheep of your pasture, will give thanks to you forever; from generation to generation we will recount your praise.
Psalm 145:4
One generation shall praise thy works to another, and shall declare thy mighty acts.

The will of God cannot be more clearly spoken than this. The Bible demands an inter-generational discourse on the Glory of God. It is incumbent upon the old and the young to worship together, to listen respectfully to each other's songs, and to seek the face of God together. There is much to learn about the lives of the elderly, the record of God's faithfulness to them, the testimony of their victories, and the amazing truth that they faced similar problems as those faced by people today. There is also much to rejoice about in the songs of the younger generations. They are singing about the same Jesus the older folks know and love! They are setting the ancient songs of heaven in their own musical languages. They are praying the same prayers using their own words and song forms. They are finding the Lord to be Savior, Friend, Healer, and Baptizer just as their parents and grandparents did. They are also looking for the same Jesus to return in their lifetimes. What's not to love?

How can we establish and maintain generational joy in public worship? It begins with the realization that Jesus wants the church to be ONE, not many.

> ### John 17:11
> And now I am no more in the world,
> but these are in the world, and I come to thee. Holy Father,
> keep through thine own name those whom thou hast given
> me, that they may be one, as we are.

How can we become the answer to the prayer of Jesus? Here are some ways.

- We must develop and perpetuate a United Vision for Public Worship.

- We must operate with a United Purpose for Worship.

- We must be a United Worship Family.

A United Vision for Public Worship

If there are 100 worshipers in your congregation there may be 100 competing sets of expectations of every worship service. The Pastor must standardize these expectations by presenting a biblical vision upon which a consensus of the congregation can be built. Until the Pastor establishes the biblical context for worship, everything will be judged by the people to be simply the preferences of the people in charge, principally the worship leader. Here is an example of a United Vision for Worship:

> ## A United Vision for Worship
> **The Whole Family Gathers as One to worship the Lord in Spirit and Truth.**
> **Worship Celebrates Our Heritage,**
> **Sustains Us in our Walk with God Today, and**
> **Leads us Boldly into Our Future.**

A United Purpose for Worship

The unified vision can be realized when the whole church agrees on the purpose of worship. This is the real key to peace among the generations. Conflicts arise when different people possess differing expectations of the same event. We must ask who the worship service is for, God or man?

- If our vision is toward mankind then, indeed, the purposes of the worship service are fellowship, discipleship, affirmation, and evangelism.
- If, on the other hand, the worship service is for God, then everything changes. Fellowship, discipleship, affirmation, and evangelism become the benefits of worship but are not the purpose of worship.

Seeing the differences between the benefits of worship and its purpose is essential to *Semper Reformanda!* I believe the true purpose of a worship service is True Worship.

A United Purpose of the Worship Service
We must Minister to the Lord,
giving Him the Glory due unto His Name.
We will do this by Worshiping in Spirit and in Truth
and by Pursuing His Glory.

We gather for the express purpose of giving unto the Lord "the glory due unto His name."[1] We meet to minister to the Lord! As we worship, He meets with us and ministers to us through the preaching of the Word and all the other events. When the whole church agrees to this purpose there will no longer be conflicting goals, competing needs, and clashing cultures. True Worship fulfills all these things.

A United Family in Worship
Each generation and each culture has its own heart-song, a certain musical language and textual message that unlocks the hearts of that generation or culture. Worship Leaders must know the heart-songs of their people if they are to lead them in True Worship.

- Older generations tend to celebrate their testimonies in song.
- The Baby Boomers tend to celebrate the majesty of God through worship.

---

1   Psalm 29:1,2

- Younger generations tend to express their feelings about God.

These simple descriptions are severe understatements and the truth about the generations in any congregation will be more complex than this. It is the job of the worship leader to discover the heart-songs of the people he/she wants to lead in worship.

Heart-songs can be easily discovered by listening to the songs they love to sing. What are they about? Do they speak about God or to God? What is the music of these songs like? Informed by these facts, the worship leader can find music for worship that engages these worshipers in praise and prayer. This is not the same thing as pandering to people as in, "throwing a bone to the old folks" by singing one of their hymns. This is a sincere desire to engage them in worship. It works the other way as well. A heart-song of a younger generation may need to be moderated somewhat to be useful to older worshipers.

This is where musical craft is an asset. If the worship leader can adapt older songs for younger worshipers by updating the music and make new songs more singable for older worshipers, these musical alterations can assist the congregation in multigenerational worship.

The exciting truth is that each generation needs to sing the heart-song of the others. We can lead all the people to enjoy songs beyond their natural preferences. We can draw from the music of all three generations so that all may participate. This pleases God. We must sing the songs that unlock hearts. So, how does the whole family come together in worship?

- by agreement on the vision for worship,
- by establishing the purpose of worship, and
- by singing each other's heart-songs.

A United Family in Worship
We must Sing the Heart-Songs
of each generation in the congregation.
This demands music skill and a consensus of purpose.

CENTERING ON JESUS

The highly effective worship team is one that is always centered on Jesus. Keeping Jesus at the center of our worship creates unity in the church. The church at Ephesus was made up of Jews and Gentiles, two completely different cultures. In the normal course of things, these people would not be friends, let alone brothers and sisters. The cultural wall between them was high and fortified with hostility. So much so that Paul called it a wall of hostility. And we think our church is divided! How did Paul and Timothy bring these waring cultures together? Paul is quick to share the secret: they centered everything on Jesus.

> **Ephesians 2:14-15 ESV**
> For he himself is our peace, who has made us both one and has broken down in his flesh the dividing wall of hostility.

Jesus is the ONE who brings us together. He tears down walls of hostility between groups and only He can. Applying this testimony to generational strife over worship, how do we keep Jesus at the center?

If we interviewed worshipers, who or what would they say is at the center? What is *really* going on when a church gathers to "worship"? Is it really all about Jesus? Or is someone or something else the real central issue? There *are* other possibilities:

- The **music** can be at the center.
- The **doctrine** of the church could be at the center.
- The **personality** of the preacher may be at the center.
- The **vision** of the church could be the central focus.
- **Denominational tradition** may occupy the central position.
- The latest **innovations** in worship techniques and emphases may be the center.
- The **tastes and culture** of the worshipers may have the central focus.

- The desperate **need of mankind** may be the true center of the worship life of a congregation.

- Perhaps even **the clock** might be at the center of some public worship services.

All of these things and many more can take the centerpiece of the worship service. When lost people observe off-center worship, they do not see a different kingdom, the Kingdom of God. They see a Christianized version of the culture they already know. This is a tragedy of the first order. The church should be a Shining City on a Hill—a holy Counter-culture.

How can the worship team avoid this? What can we do to make sure that Jesus is the obvious center of the worship we lead? How do we put Jesus at the Center?

- Tell His story! This is the Gospel that changes lives forever.

- Teach His truths. Every issue of contemporary life can be approached from the teachings of Jesus.

- Walk through His earthly life. The Christian Year[1] helps the whole church do this together in private and public worship.

- Sing songs about God, the Father, Son, and the Holy Spirit, not just about us and how we feel about God and what we are doing or plan to do for Him.

- Strip away the nonessentials in public worship; reduce it down to Spirit and Truth.

If walls of hostility exist in your church, Jesus is the ONE who can bring them down.

---

1   The Christian Year refers to the ancient practice of taking half the year to walk through the life of Christ: Advent, Christmas, Epiphany, Lent, Eastertide, Pentecost, and Christ the King. The other half of the year is called Kingdomtide wherein we walk out the life of Christ.

CONCLUSION

The Reformation of Worship must continue from generation to generation with an emphasis on the Lord Jesus. Worship leaders and pastors must regularly and fearlessly examine their thinking and their practice to see if culture is being canonized—given an undue place of authority. To do this, a clear understanding of what is eternal and what is temporary is needed.

Semper Reformanda! is the process of holding on and letting go: holding on to the eternal and letting go of the temporary when its time is done. The Truths we all hold dear unite us:

- Jesus is Savior, King, Friend, and God is our Father;
- The Bible is the Word of God;
- The Holy Spirit is our Helper;
- Jesus is Coming Again;
- We are the People of God created to worship Him.

Our cultural expressions are differences to be celebrated:

- young people listening to the musical testimonies of their elders and
- old people rejoicing in the new songs of their children and grandchildren.

"From generation to generation we will recount Your praise."[1]

---

1   Psalm 79:13 ESV

DISCUSSION QUESTIONS

1. Discuss how a move of God affects the generations.

2. What is meant by Unity with Diversity?

3. What does Semper Reformanda! mean to you?

4. How have you experienced "traditioning" in the church?

5. Is it really possible for there to be an inter-generational discourse on worship?

6. How would you describe a United Family in Worship?

7. What things or people can become the center of worship?

With Jesus at the Center of Our Lives, Worship Is Certainly More than Music!

Postlude

Romans 12:1
I beseech you therefore, brethren, by the mercies of God, that ye present your bodies a living sacrifice, holy, acceptable unto God, which is your reasonable service.
("your spiritual Worship" ESV)

Colossians 3:17, 23-24
And whatsoever ye do in word or deed, do all in the name of the Lord Jesus, giving thanks to God and the Father by him. And whatsoever ye do, do it heartily, as to the Lord, and not unto men; Knowing that of the Lord ye shall receive the reward of the inheritance: for ye serve the Lord Christ.

A Coin with Two Sides

Different translations of the Bible will render Romans 12:1 as both worship and service. The reason for this is the meaning of the original Greek word, *latreia*.[1] It is a direct reference to the service given by priests in the Temple to the Lord—their service was worship. Modern thinking tends to separate these two things into competing categories. Sometimes this is posted on signs at churches: "Enter to Worship—Exit to Serve."

---

1   Strong's Concordance

This false dichotomy hinders our understanding of what we are doing when we worship the Lord in church and when we follow Him in our daily lives. Here is the fullness of the truth:

> **When we are worshiping God,**
> **we are serving Him.**
> **When we are serving God,**
> **we are worshiping Him.**[1]

This is a treasure coin with two valuable sides! Worship Team members must understand the transformation this brings to all aspects of this ministry.

- Services, warm-ups, sound checks are all of equal value.
- Personal preparation between events becomes a personal altar.
- Relationships among team members are a mirror of each member's relationship with God.
- Issues of the heart, known only to God, are as important as issues of artistry and presentation.

The Call on our Lives

In the beginning, we dealt with the Call to Worship and now we see that it is also a Call to Serve. Worship Team members are not star performers on stage before an audience. They are priests unto the Lord leading the People of God in the Living Sacrifice of Praise. They must worship the Lord as they are serving Him. Paul gives us the secret of this life of total worship/service to God. I call it the Colossians Credo. It employs the most inclusive word possible—"whatsoever." This word extends the truth of this command well beyond the sanctuary to the details and drudgeries of life. The members of a highly effective worship team are servants of the Lord.

1   Phifer, Stephen R. *Worship that Pleases God: The Passion and Reason of True Worship* Trafford Publishing Company, 2005 p. 71

> ## The Colossians Credo
> ### *Whatsoever ye do in word or deed,*
> ### *do all in the name of the Lord Jesus,*
> ### *giving thanks to God and the Father by him.*
> ### *And whatsoever ye do, do it heartily,*
> ### *as to the Lord, and not unto men.*
> **Colossians 3:17; 23-24**

With this creed, work becomes worship and worship becomes work. Remember that worship is God's Dwelling Place. He is enthroned upon worship and He inhabits it. That means that all of life can be worship to the Lord. We can live, work, play and rest all in the name of Jesus, with thanksgiving, with all our might, and as unto God, and not unto men.

Now Go Serve Him as You Worship Him!

We are servants, not stars; priests, not performers; called not coerced; humble not proud; and God gives us grace. Serve Him and worship Him with rehearsals and services, with voices and instruments, with technologies and willing hearts. This is important work! This is worship that is vital. This is the Glory due His name and it is the hope of the world.

Dr. Stephen Phifer,

Let Our Worship Be More than Music!

Supplemental Resources

I strongly suggest worship team members take advantage of my online resources.

• PathofLifeDevotions.com is a daily devotion designed to aid prayer "in the Secret Place." While not specifically addressing worship team issues, these devotions are an attempt to present inspirational truths to aid in the team members' walk with God.

• StevePhifer.com is the internet presence of The Worship Renewal Center. This is a growing library of articles and other resources concerning issues and principles of worship renewal. The several hundred articles are easily accessed by an index by category and title. If team members want to explore topics introduced in "Much More then Music," they can find more information at StevePhifer.com.

• *Worship that Pleases God: The Passion and Reason of True Worship* is the product of ten years of biblical study and more than 20 years of ministry experience in leading worship. This major text goes into greater detail on the Seven Biblical Models of Worship and the biblical worship vocabulary. The premise of the book is that True Worship establishes the Kingdom of God among us. The Kingdom is described in scripture as "Righteousness, Peace, and Joy in the Holy Spirit." These qualities are the titles of the three sections of the book. In this way, "Worship that Pleases God," extends far beyond the sanctuary to the private altar, the home, and even to the workplace. In each of these venues, true worship by the Christ-follower establishes the Kingdom of God in our lives The book is available from Amazon.com in paperback, Kindle, and digital forms.

My Prayer for You

To me, the issues of worship renewal amount to an emergency; we must be about the Master's business. The time is too short for the singers, instrumentalists, and technicians who are called to lead the church in worship to be distracted by lesser things or even encumbered by shallow spirituality. We need highly effective worship teams! There is power—that of the Holy Spirit—available to rest upon the public art we create and lead. "The Brooding Dove of Heaven," as previous generations spoke of the Spirit, comes to rest upon those who are making their art from the heart out, hearts cleansed by Calvary's stream and refined by the Fire of the Spirit.

There is so much at stake. In the last days, two biblical prophecies are predicted to happen at the same time:

1. The Great Falling Away (II Thessalonians 2:3) with "perilous times" (II Timothy 3:1) and a spirit of lawlessness (Matthew 24:12), and,

2. The Great Outpouring of the Holy Spirit when the Lord floods the earth with the power of the Holy Spirit. (Joel 2:28-32 and Acts 14:21)

These are the forces behind the daily news that confronts us every day. Our choice is clear: Will we join the apostasy? The Great Falling Away? Or will we seek to be blessed by the Great Outpouring of the Holy Spirit?

The Choice Is Ours.

Every day, when we choose the Secret Place and time with the Father, we choose the Outpouring. Every week when the team gathers to rehearse our public art, we are choosing the Outpouring.

Every service, when the countdown is done and the click track counts us off, we are choosing the outpouring. The highly effective worship team is the one lifting up the praise of God, the name Jesus, and opening their hearts to the ministry of the Spirit. We are offering hope, the only true hope, to our corner of this fallen world.

God has not called us to failure but to highly effective ministry! From hearts set aflame by the Holy Spirit, and human frames prepared by diligence to be skillful, the Lord will shine forth. As the Psalmist predicts, "Out of Zion, the perfection of beauty, God shines forth!" (Psalm 50:2 ESV) True worship is the hope of this fallen world.

It is no wonder that worship is More than Music!

About The Author

Steve Phifer is a third generation Assemblies of God minister with family roots going back to the founding decade of the Pentecostal movement. At age 15, he felt a call to a life in music and at age 17 received a call to preach. He abandoned a life in music and made plans to train to be a pastor. The Lord had other plans for him.

Through miraculous circumstances and through open and closed doors, Steve decided that both calls were valid and he accepted music scholarships at Arkansas A&M College in the fall of 1967. In the summer of 1968, he applied for and received his initial ministerial recognition with the Arkansas Assemblies of God. After graduation with a BME in June 1971, he accepted a band director position at his hometown high school. Steve and his parents also began a traveling preaching and singing ministry as, "The Phifers."

It was through this ministry that Steve met Freeda Woolf, a music major at the University of Central Arkansas. They married in June 1974 and began full-time ministry in June of 1975. They served churches in Camden and North Little Rock before moving to Kansas.

In 1980, after 9 years of teaching and music ministry leadership, Steve became the principle worship leader for Bethel Life Center in Wichita, KS. While serving there, Steve began work on a Masters of Music Education at Wichita State University. In 1984 they moved to Winston-Salem to serve as Worship Pastor at First Assembly of God in that city. He finished his masters in 1986 and found himself deep in the biblical study of Worship. That work eventually became his book, "Worship that Pleases God: the Passion and Reason of True Worship." His work in his 30s and early 40s consumed most of his creative energy because of the tremendous move of God at that church. In 1993, Steve was tapped as Field Representative for Worship Arts for the Assemblies of God and in 1995 he answered the call to join the music faculty of Southeastern Assemblies of God College in Lakeland, FL. Soon, he felt the call back into local church leadership for another 10 years serving Suncoast Cathedral in St Petersburg, FL and Word of Life International Church in Springfield, VA. He earned the Doctor of Worship Studies degree from The Robert E. Webber Institute for Worship Studies in 2004. He was the first Classical Pentecostal to finish this degree.

In 2008, 40 years after becoming a credential minister, Steve retired from church staff ministry to write and teach biblical concepts of worship and worship leading. He formed The Worship Renewal Center as a website presence for his writing: StevePhifer.com. In 2008 Steve and Dr. Billy DeSanto of the University of Valley Forge in PA designed the Master of Arts in Worship Studies degree. Steve authored and teaches these classes: Introduction to Worship Studies, Biblical Foundations of Worship, Pentecostal Spirituality, Developing and Leading the Worship Team, Pastoring the Worshiping Community, and Lead Pastor--Lead Worshiper. In 2017, Steve completed a full year of daily devotions published at PathofLifeDevotions.com. In 2018 he plans to publish a full year of devotions called "The Jesus Story."

Freeda is an accomplished pianist, musical theatre director, and music educator. She and Steve have two daughters who married two outstanding young men of God: Matt and Nicole Huett of North Carolina and Manny and Jennifer Foret of Florida. They have two delightful grandsons, Charlie and Samuel Foret.

Endorsements for Dr. Stephen Phifer

"Steve Phifer has a wonderful heart for ministry and a passion for worship renewal. I have found him to be articulate and convicting about his insight on the direction of worship ministry in the 21st century." ~ **Vern Sanders, Publisher, CREATOR Magazine.**

"Dr. Steve Phifer is a gifted speaker who communicates with great passion. His years of scholarship and ministry experience in the area of worship results in anointed presentations. His seminars are always relevant because they focus on the unchanging truths found in the Scriptures. I highly recommend his ministry to your worship team and congregation!" ~ **Dr. Billy DeSanto Chair, Music Department – University of Valley Forge.**

"Steve Phifer has impacted so many lives through the years, including mine. His knowledge of the Word of God, his musical expertise, and his passion for serving Jesus and others make for a powerful combination in helping the world experience God." ~ **Michael Neale, Dove Award-Winning Songwriter, National Best-Selling Author and Lead Worship Pastor of Prestonwood Baptist Church in Plano, TX.**

"Dr. Stephen Phifer has turned into my go-to window when I want to look into the world of Pentecostal worship. He brings to the academic task a solid, integrative perspective born from decades of experience in worship leadership, a biblical sensitivity, and a willingness to learn from the broader Christian tradition." ~ **Dr. Lester Ruth, Research Professor of Christian Worship, Duke Divinity School, Durham, North Carolina.**

"Dr. Steve Phifer is one of those guys that you quickly realize has a sincere and caring desire for what he teaches, writes, and all around exhorts. His book, Worship That Pleases God, quickly became one of my favorites in the beginning of my doctoral studies. His understanding and expertise on the subject of worship is one to be 'taken advantage of.'" ~ **Luke Gambill. Assistant Professor of Music/Coordinator of Contemporary Worship, William Carey University.**

"I have been blessed many times over with the wisdom and knowledge of Steve Phifer's writings and teachings. He is a solid man of faith, the Word, and wisdom. EVERYONE will benefit from this ministry. It is a must have resource!" ~ **Rev. Cyd Collischonn, Director of Creative Arts, Calvary Assembly of God, Cobleskill, MY.**

"Depth of scripture, depth of thought and depth of passion are rare commodities these days, and even more rare to find all three embodied in one individual. With now 30 years of journey, I have never not (sorry Steve, double negative just says it best) experienced the evidence of all three in the words and writings of Dr. Steve Phifer." ~ **John R. Bost, President Master Counsel & Associates, Inc.**

"Dr. Steve Phifer is a man after God's own heart, loving God with all he has within him. He epitomizes the concept of a "kneeing theology," doing theological reflection from an attitude of prayer and devotion, with a heart of worship. There is no better endorsement and no higher calling. He leads a straight path to the throne of God that is paved with prayer and praise. His unique style will grab your attention and beg for more. I encourage you to open the door for his ministry at your church." ~ **Bob Brock, President/Founder, Compassion in Action.**

Dr. Stephen Phifer is the consummate pastoral musician. Throughout his multi-faceted ministry career he has served as worship leader, arranger, conductor, author, professor and, perhaps more relevant, distinguished mentor. He is widely regarded for his presence on social media. That said, I would like to emphasis not only his prolific scholarship but his care and concern for our fellow guides into the presence of the LORD. Clearly Dr. Phifer understands the Biblical presupposition, "It's not by might not by power, but by the Spirit," says the Lord of Hosts. I urge you to check out his writings for they will not only enrich your life but augment your ministry effectiveness. ~ **Tom McDonald, Ph.D. Los Angeles, CA.**

Dr. Steve Phifer is an accomplished musician and gifted teacher, with a deep insight into Biblical concepts of worship. I have enjoyed hearing him deliver these truths in a personal style that includes a quick wit and knowledge of history...I highly recommend Dr. Steve Phifer! ~ **Darlene Greenlee, CTN Network Producer-Host**.

Dear Reader,

If you were blessed by *More than Music; Becoming a Highly Effective Worship Team*, help spread the word about this great tool by sharing this book on your social media profiles and by reviewing this book on the retail site where it was purchased.

To receive email notifications concerning future books from this author and Empowered Publications sign up for our newsletter at empowered.news .

Additional copies are available at www.filledbooks.com.

Many Blessings,

The Team at Empowered Publications

EMPOWERED
PUBLICATIONS INC.